The

Internet
FOR BUSY PEOPLE

Christian Crumlish

Osborne/**McGraw-Hill**

Berkeley / New York / St. Louis / San Francisco / Auckland / Bogotá
Hamburg / London / Madrid / Mexico City / Milan / Montreal / New Delhi
Panama City / Paris / São Paulo / Singapore / Sydney / Tokyo / Toronto

Osborne/**McGraw-Hill**
2600 Tenth Street
Berkeley, California 94710
U.S.A.

For information on translations or book distributors outside the U.S.A., or to arrange bulk purchase discounts for sales promotions, premiums, or fundraisers, please contact Osborne/**McGraw-Hill** at the above address.

The Internet for Busy People

234567890 DOC 99876

ISBN 0-07-882108-8

Publisher: Lawrence Levitsky
Acquisitions Editor: Joanne Cuthbertson
Project Editor: Bob Myren
Copy Editor: Ann Spivack
Proofreader: Bill Cassel
Graphic Artist: Marla J. Shelasky
Computer Designers: Leslee Bassin, Roberta Steele
Quality Control: Joe Scuderi
Series and Cover Design: Ted Mader Associates
Series Illustration: Daniel Barbeau

To Briggs, one of the busiest people I know.

Contents at a glance

Contents

ACKNOWLEDGMENTS

Everyone involved in this project performed at an amazing level of cooperation, sympathy, and communication. Larry Levitsky conceived of this series, creating a vision that the rest of us all executed. Joanne Cuthbertson recruited me and fellow-author Ron Mansfield and gave us unprecedented guidance in the early thematic, conceptual, and design stages of the books. Without her continuing insight and influence, these books could never have been made.

Right down the line, the Osborne team pulled out all the stops for this book and I'm heartily grateful (Executive Editor, Scott Rogers; Marketing Manager, Kendal Andersen; Editorial Assistant, Heidi Poulin, thank you!). Before I had written a word (well, maybe a sample chapter or two), Ted Mader's witty, sophisticated design, built around Dan Barbeau's frazzled, contemporary people-oids, set the tone for the project and kept my mind on you, the kind of person who needs a book like this.

Copyeditor Ann Spivack made sure I didn't drift off too far into the lands of high-falutin' slang and jargon, and made sure I finished my sentences. Project Editor Bob Myren was an absolute pleasure to work with. His witty queries and comments in the manuscript made the editing process as enjoyable as a good correspondence. He synthesized Ann's queries with his own and generally streamlined all the processes, making this book possible on schedules that on paper look totally impossible.

Technical Editor Malcolm Humes is a hero of this book. More than a fact and detail checker, Mal made pertinent and sometimes challenging suggestions at various crucial points throughout the manuscript, all of which raised the standards of the material within and gave my own expertise a shot in the arm. Malcolm Humes: Guru Helper.

By the time I sat down to write this book, I had just finished another book in the same vein, *Word for Busy People*, and the Osborne production crew had had at least a little time to work out some of the wrinkles inherent in making a book with a new kind of design. Then again, we all had two or three fewer weeks to produce the same amount of work in (see we're all bona fide busy people ourselves!), so the race was on once again. The art and production team, headed by Marla Shelasky and including Roberta Steele, Leslee Bassin, Lance Ravella, Peter H. Hancik, Richard Whitaker, and quality control specialist Joe Scuderi, produced the pages so deftly that I rarely had more than a comment or two before they were finalized.

Thanks to the military-industrial complex for underwriting the Internet in the early days. Thanks to all of the active citizens of the Net who are busy volunteering their time and information and building communities based on communication. Thanks to Briggs, geebers, my family, the Enterzone gang, Levi, the antiweb list, the pink light, Canopus, the OTISts, and many more.

Oh, and I'm convinced that proofreader Bill Cassel has secretly embedded deliberate errors in this manuscript but I can't find them, I tell you.

INTRODUCTION

When Osborne/McGraw-Hill publisher Larry Levitsky described to me his idea for a new computer book series "for busy people," I knew he was onto something. As I worked on this book, it seemed like every day I was hearing some friend or acquaintance talk about how busy they'd become, how their jobs had mushroomed into sprawling layers of responsibility, how they had almost no time for anything. If I had any doubts (and my own hectic schedule was enough to convince me!) I was sure that there must be many people out there with only a night or a few lunch hours to learn how to explore the Internet.

The "digital revolution" has given with one hand, creating all kinds of rapid means of electronic communication, and taken away with the other, accelerating everyone's expectations, constantly moving the goalposts. For many, life has become a treadmill with someone quickening the pace each day. How often do people say to you "Fax me that draft," or "e-mail me those statistics," "our product release deadline's been moved up due to competitive pressures," or "it took longer than we thought—can you make up the time at your end?"

To help you meet your needs, my editor, Joanne Cuthbertson, demanded opinionated, thoughtfully organized writing with a touch of skepticism. With Windows 95's new support for Internet connections, I was itching to write an Internet book geared towards that operating system (but useable by anyone), so it was a perfect match.

I KNOW YOU'RE IN A HURRY, SO...

Let's agree to dispense with the traditional computer book preliminaries. You've probably used a mouse, held down two keys at once, and have heard of this vast global network called the Internet. If you don't yet have Internet access, or if you're not sure what type of connection might already be available to you, start off by flipping to Appendix A, where I explain the different types of connections and how to find and select an Internet service provider (ISP).

So, now lets cut to the chase. After reading the first few chapters, you'll be able to:

- Browse the World Wide Web
- Send, receive, and reply to e-mail
- Find and join electronic mailing lists
- Subscribe to Usenet newsgroups (discussion groups) and join online IRC chats.

Later chapters will show you how to transfer files from Internet archive sites to your home (or office) computer, how to log into other computers on the Internet, how to use a Gopher program to explore menu-driven Gopher sites. You'll also learn some easy ways to search the Internet and I'll give you a starter set of Web addresses to explore. The last chapter, Chapter 12, can get you started publishing on the World Wide Web.

If you're curious about the Microsoft Network (MSN) icon on the Windows 95 desktop, you can get help signing up and an orientation to this new online service in Appendix B. You don't need MSN access to to use this book, but if you aren't yet connected to the Internet, MSN is one way to explore it.

Throughout this book, I suggest World Wide Web addresses (also called URLs) that you can visit for more information or to obtain free Internet programs and other software. All of the Web addresses in this book are collected for your easy reference in Appendix C (as well as online at http://syx.com/x/busy/).

ACCESSING THE INTERNET WITH WINDOWS 95 OR OTHER COMPUTERS

This book uses examples and illustrations showing the Windows 95 versions of most Internet programs and features, but most of the information in the book applies equally well to other types of computers and operating systems, including earlier versions of Windows and even Macintosh and UNIX systems. For other operating systems, you'll sometimes have to download different software or different versions of the programs I mention. Appendices A and C will also help you in setting up or working with a non-Windows 95 Internet connection.

THINGS YOU MIGHT WANT TO KNOW ABOUT THIS BOOK

You can read this book more or less in any order. I suggest cruising Chapter 1 and reading Chapter 2 first, but you can start just as easily with Chapter 3 and 4 (which deal with e-mail) or by jumping ahead to Chapters 10 and 11 to start right off exploring and searching the Web. Use the book as a reference. When you're stuck, not sure how to do something, know there's an answer but not what it is, pick up the book, zero in on the answer to your question, and put the book down again. Besides clear, coherent explanations of this all-over-the-map network of networks, you'll also find some special elements to help you get the most out of the Internet. Here's a quick run down of the other elements in this book.

Fast Forwards

Each chapter begins with a section called *Fast Forward*. They should always be your first stop if you are a confident user, or impatient or habitually late. You might find everything you need to get back in stride. Think of them as the *Reader's Digest* version of each chapter. This shorthand may leave you hungry, especially if you are new to the Internet. So, for more complete and leisurely explanations of techniques and shortcuts, read the rest of the chapter.

Fast Forwards are, in effect, a book within a book—a built-in quick reference guide, summarizing the key tasks explained in each chapter.

If you're a fast learner, or somewhat experienced, this may be the only material you need. Written step-by-step, point-by-point, there are also page references to guide you to the more complete information later in the chapter.

Habits & Strategies

Habits & Strategies suggest timesaving tips, techniques, and worthwhile addictions. (Look for the man at the chessboard.) Force yourself to develop some good habits now, when it's still possible! These sidebars also give you the big picture and help you plan ahead. For example, I'll suggest that you use an "off-line" newreader program to save on connect-time charges while reading Usenet newsgroups.

Shortcuts

Shortcuts are designed for the busy person—when there's a way to do something that may not be as full-featured as the material in the text, but is *faster*, it will show up in the margin, below the business man leaping over a fence.

Cautions

Sometimes it's too easy to plunge ahead and fall down a rabbit hole, resulting in hours of extra work just to get you back to where you were before you went astray. This hardhat will warn you before you commit time-consuming mistakes.

Definitions

Usually, I explain computer or networking jargon in the text, wherever the technobabble first occurs. But if you encounter words you don't recognize, look for this body builder in the margin. *Definitions* point out important terms you reasonably might not know the meaning of. When necessary they're strict and a little technical, but most of the time they're informal and conversational.

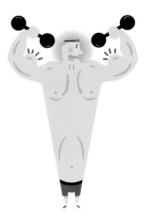

Throughout the book, cross-references and other minor asides appear in the margins.

Netiquette

There are some well-established guidelines for behavior on the Internet, most often referred to as *netiquette*, that keep the Net cooperative and help everyone get along. Civility and familiarity with the traditional ways of doing things go a long way in helping you communicate with the total strangers you'll meet online. Netiquette boxes will tip you off to standard practices and *faux pas* to avoid.

Web Addresses

World Wide Web addresses, also called URLs, are notoriously long and strangely punctuated. Often, a Web address will not fit on a single line of text. To avoid introducing spurious characters that will make the addresses actually incorrect, Web addresses are "wrapped" without hyphens or any other special characters added, usually after a slash (/) or dot (.) character. So for example, to point your Web browser at http://enterzone.berkeley.edu/enterzone.html, just type the entire address on one line without any spaces or breaks (and don't type the comma at the end—that's just part of this sentence).

LET'S DO IT!

Ready? Let's dive into the Internet before the next big thing comes along!

Incidentally, I'm always happy to hear your reactions to this or any of my other books. You can reach me through the publisher or on the Net (*xian@syx.com*).

CHAPTER

1

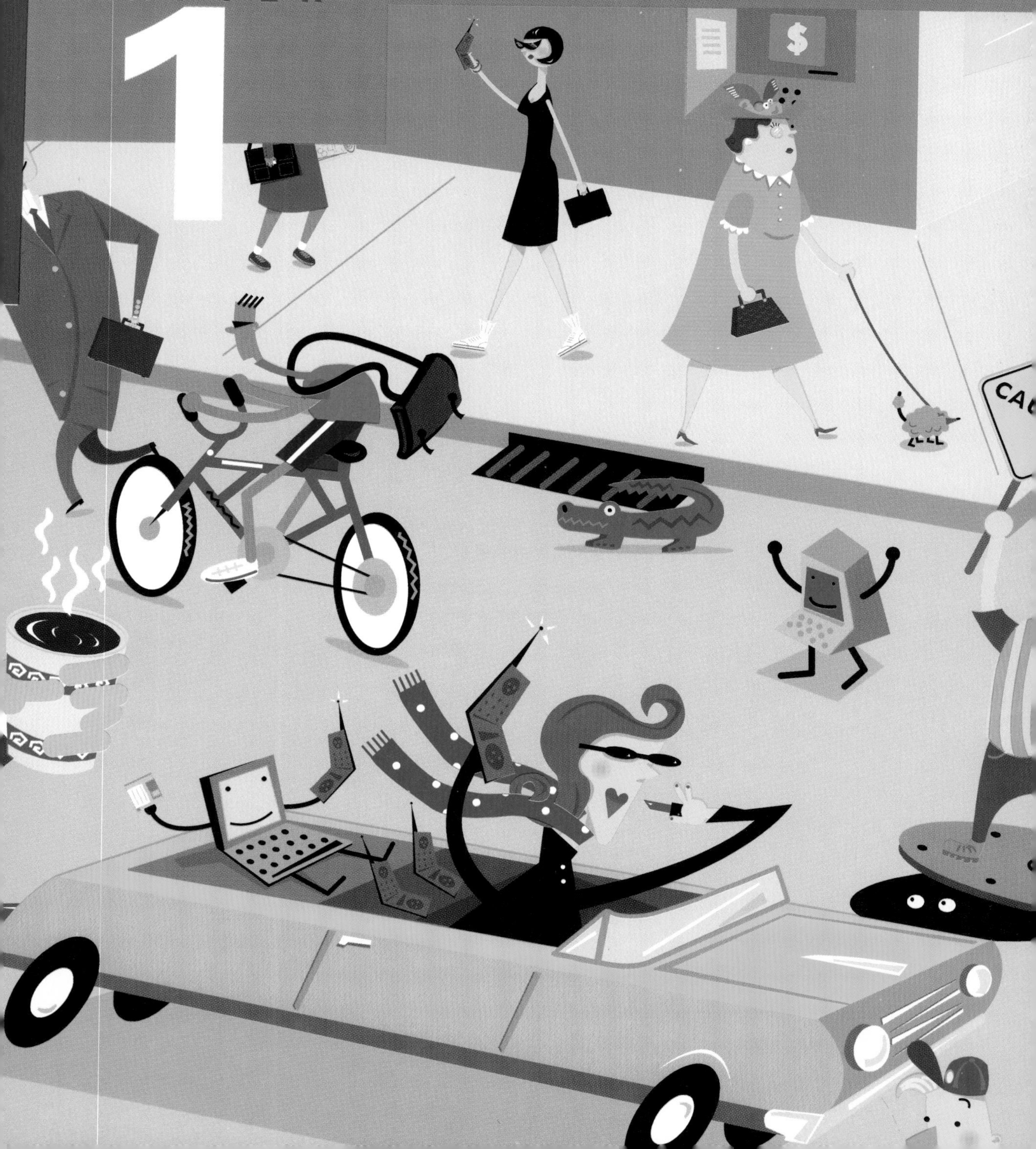

The World Wide Web: Click Here!

1

FAST FORWARD

WHAT IS THE INTERNET? ➤ *pp 4-5*

The Internet is a loosely and redundantly linked collection of smaller networks and individual computers, all of which agree to share (some) information using the various Internet protocols as a *lingua franca*.

HOW DO WEB ADDRESSES WORK? ➤ *pp 5-6*

Web addresses (also called URLs) can be long and difficult to remember.

- Whenever possible, avoid typing them in by hand.
- When copying by hand, be very careful to copy them exactly.

BROWSE THE WEB ➤ *pp 6-11*

Most of the time, you'll browse by pointing to and clicking hyperlinks, specially highlighted text or images that lead your Web browser to a new destination.

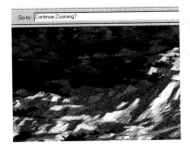

WHAT WILL THE WEB
LOOK LIKE TOMORROW? ➤ *p 8*

Most destinations on the Web today can be thought of as documents. In the future, Web sites may behave more like places or programs.

WHEN YOUR BROWSER
FAILS TO CONNECT TO A SITE ➤ *pp 11-12*

Don't worry about it. The Internet is sometimes "busy." Click the Stop button and try again. If you fail to connect repeatedly, try again later.

USE THE WEB WITHOUT WASTING TIME ➤ *pp 12-13*

- Keep a goal or destination in mind.
- Save references to interesting destinations for those occasions when you have the leisure to browse freely.

It's only recently become possible for a busy person to check out the Internet. Up to very recently, you had to deal with arcane, computer-science "protocols," and usually the powerful but willfully obscure UNIX operating system. That has all changed recently. First commercial online services started creating "gateways" to the Internet, and now direct Internet access—via a network, Internet service provider, or online service—is commonplace and easy to use.

In the near future, the Web may also become the easiest and most direct way to buy or sell things on the Internet.

THE WEB MAKES THE INTERNET EASY TO GET AROUND

The most important advance in making the Internet easy and convenient to explore has been the development of the World Wide Web, a subset of the Internet, and elegant programs called Web browsers that enable you to view and thumb through the myriad sources of information, communication, and software out there.

Now, "browsing" the Internet is a simple matter of running one of these programs and jumping to a destination. Because of the flexibility of the Web medium, you can even use a Web browser to gain access to items that are on the Internet but not on the Web. The Web browser acts as a sort of umbrella interface for the entire Internet.

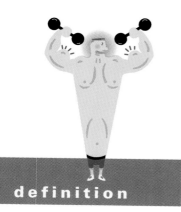

definition

protocol: A protocol is an agreed-upon method of communication, but don't worry about it.

A NETWORK OF NETWORKS

We're both too busy to spend all day discussing the history and computer science of the Internet and all the fascinating trivia associated with it. You can get those anecdotes anywhere. (For that matter, you can get them for free once you're on the Net.) Suffice it to say that the Internet is not really a coherent network in the sense of an office's "local-area network" or a campus'"wide-area network." Actually, the Internet is a loosely and redundantly linked agglomeration of smaller networks and individual computers, all of which agree to share (some) information using the various Internet protocols as a *lingua franca*.

When people talk about "addresses" on the Internet, they usually mean Web addresses (URLs) or e-mail addresses (see Chapter 3).

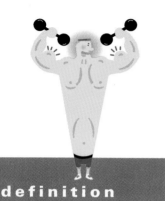

definition

URL: Stands for "universal resource locator," but really just means an Internet address expressed in a form that any Web browser can understand. Web addresses usually start with http:// (or something else://) and usually end with .html or just a trailing / to indicate the default file in a folder.

If you ask what the Internet is like or how it works, you'll get the sort of range of answers obtainable from blind men touching an elephant. The Internet is like a cloud. The Internet is like a web. The Internet is like a tree. I suggest you think of the Internet as a "black box." Stuff goes in one end and comes out the other and forget trying to figure out what happens in the middle. Why did the chicken choose a particular path through the Internet? To get to the other side.

WEB ADDRESSES

In a perfect Internet, every interesting destination on the World Wide Web would be accessible via a single click of the mouse. Because the Net evolves so quickly, though, there is no single comprehensive listing anywhere that covers everything you might ever want to see. Sometimes, you'll hear about an interesting spot on the Web from a book or newspaper article, or even from a friend. In that case, the location on the Web will be expressed in the form of a *URL*.

Here are four sample URLs:

```
http://yahoo.com
http://enterzone.berkeley.edu/enterzone.html
gopher://garnet.msen.com:70/11/stuff/gutenberg
news://news.announce.newusers
```

The first URL points to the main page (also called the index or default file) on the Yahoo server. (Yahoo is a huge directory of Internet resources accessible via the Web). The second one points to the home page—the primary Web document—of a magazine called *Enterzone*, on a server also called Enterzone in the domain of the University of California at Berkeley. The third one points to a menu on a Gopher server, which is technically not a Web document but which can be reached via the Web, on a machine on the network of MSEN, an Internet service provider. The last one is the address of a Usenet newsgroup. Generally, though, as a rule of thumb, a given address corresponds to a specific document somewhere out there on the Internet.

Don't worry about learning the system for URLs. Before long, they'll always be completely hidden. For now, just be sure to spell them right, carefully copying a URL character for character (and making sure

Gopher will be explained in Chapter 9. We'll get to Usenet in Chapter 6.

to duplicate capitalization as well—parts of URLs are case-sensitive), if you plan to use it to reach a destination.

If you *are* forced to copy a Web address off paper, beware of some common typographical errors. Web addresses rarely end in periods, for example, so if you see an address printed with a period at the end, it's probably just punctuation in the sentence and not part of the address. They do often end in the letters "html" or with a forward slash (/) (minus the quotation marks, naturally). Web addresses sometimes have a ~ character (called a tilde) in them, and some newspapers will mess up and put that symbol on top of a letter of the alphabet instead of before it.

In Windows 95, it's possible for someone to send you e-mail with an attached Web address so that all you have to do is double-click the attachment and Windows will start up your Web browser (Microsoft's Internet Explorer by default) and go directly to the attached address.

FORGET ADDRESSES, JUST CLICK AND GO

Fortunately, most of the time you'll be able to get around the Web just fine by following links. What are links? Links are parts of a document—sometimes text, sometimes pictures—that lead to other documents, to other parts of the same document, or to other destinations on the Web entirely. They're really embedded URLs, embedded Web addresses that you can click on. The organizing structure (such as it is) of the Web is composed of these so-called hyperlinks.

Traditionally (on the Web, that means since 1993), link text in Web browsers appears blue (instead of black) and is underlined. Link pictures usually have a blue border. Your mouse pointer changes when you place it over a link. More and more Web pages are using customized colors, though, so you can't count on blue meaning link. Also, I usually turn off link underlining as I find it often looks ugly, and some link pictures have invisible borders. Ultimately, the only consistent evidence of a link is that it will change the appearance of your mouse pointer when you point to one.

Find out

To compare advertisements on the Web to those on television, some people speak of a "pull" vs. "push" metaphor; TV ads are pushed toward you, but Web ads pull you toward them, giving you more control.

More and more pages are beginning to sport "image maps," which are clickable images that connect to different URLs depending on where you click on the image.

On the Beaten Track

The Web is a weird conglomeration of major media outlets, underground or alternative publishing ventures, self-promotion, home movies, and billboards. Amidst all this chaos are some big players, usually tied to major publishing empires and supported by advertising. One nice thing about advertising on the Web is that you can generally avoid it simply by not clicking on the links to sponsors' sites. On the other hand, you'll be forced to see (and wait for) the art associated with the link when a Web page including an ad is loaded.

The Web browser you use determines where you start (what home page you start on), and therefore what primary links are available to you and whose list of cool or new sites you see.

Some of the big names or owners of major pages you'll hear about include Netscape (makers of the most widely distributed browser), Yahoo (one of the most comprehensive directories), *HotWired* (the first major commercial Web publication), PathFinder (Time/Warner's Web site), NCSA (distributors of Mosaic, the first graphical browser to really spark the growth of the Web), and CERN (the lab in Switzerland where the Web protocols were designed), among others. You'll find these sites with no trouble, because all roads lead to them.

Off the Beaten Track

Because the Web is so chaotic and formless, the big boys share shelf space with independent Web artists, personal confession pages, grass roots projects, and so on. These links aren't always as well publicized or easy to find, but a lot of them tend to link to each other in a sort of noncommercial underground Web or "antiweb," so once you find your way into the boho districts of the Web, you can easily navigate from there.

Other items accessible via the Web, such as Gopher menus, are technically not real Web pages, and therefore lack the facility to fully incorporate links to other Web pages. Because of this, they generally function as cul-de-sacs, and you'll need to use your Back button to retreat from them back onto the Web proper.

habits & strategies

You can always customize the home page of a browser to point to your own personal favorite page or list of sites, as explained in Chapter 2.

THE FUTURE OF THE WEB

For now, almost everything on the Web can be thought of as a "document," using something similar to the model of a piece of paper. (Hence the "page" metaphor used all over the Web.) This document model might be changing, as new technologies such as HotJava (a Sun scripting language that would allow people to run interactive programs over the Web) and VRML (Virtual Reality Modeling Language, a method of describing three-dimensional spaces that people could navigate with special browsers, not unlike the way people now play DOOM and other 3-D shoot-em-up games) begin to emerge.

For the immediate future, though, the document model with hyperlinks should continue to dominate the field. In some ways, the less you know about all this the better. The advances that succeed will make the Web even easier and more transparent to navigate, integrating it more closely with graphical user interfaces.

JARGON TO WATCH OUT FOR

Just to satisfy your curiosity, I'll give you a short briefing on the jargon you'll encounter on the Web (and the Net) in Table1.1, but don't let the terminology get in your way. The point is to sit back and browse, following your own instincts. Let the geeks and gurus yak in the lingo.

Jargon Term	What It Means
bookmark	Also called a hotlist entry or favorite place, a saved link to a Web address.
browser	A program used to connect to sites on the World Wide Web.
client	A program, such as a Web browser, that connects to a centralized server program and obtains information from it.
client/server model	A method of sharing computer and network resources by centralizing some functions with a server and allowing individual clients to connect to the server to perform those functions.
home page	A major or central document at a World Wide Web site.
HTML	(Hypertext markup language.) The language (consisting mainly of "tags") used to format a document for the World Wide Web, including both structural formatting and hyperlinks.

Table 1.4 World Wide Web Jargon

Jargon Term	What It Means
HTTP	(Hypertext transport protocol.) The technique used by Web servers to dispense information to Web browsers.
hyper	Nonlinear, capable of branching off in many directions. (Can be used alone or as a prefix.)
image map	A clickable image that connects to different URLs depending on which part of the image is clicked.
Information Superhighway, Infoway, Infobahn, Info Highway, etc.	The terms correspond to nothing in the real world. The Internet is not a superhighway. The terms were coined to describe a possible information infrastructure, using coaxial or fiber-optic cables, that would upgrade the existing system.
Internet	A collection of networks and computers all over the world, all of which share information, or at least e-mail, by agreed-upon Internet protocols.
link	A specially designated word or image that, when selected, takes a Web browser to a new page or other destination (an embedded Web address).
multimedia	Incorporating many different media, often including text, pictures, sounds, video, animations, and so on.
Net	A loosely defined term meant to suggest the loose association of all or most computers on the planet. Generally refers to a more inclusive set of linked networks than just the Internet, but also corresponds roughly to the Internet.
page	On the World Wide Web, an HTML document.
server	A piece of software or machine that acts as a centralized source of information or computing resouces (such as Web sites, Gopher menus, FTP archives, and so on), available to clients.
site	A location on the Internet, often the host of one or more servers, or a set of related Web pages, also sometimes called a webspace.
Web	The World Wide Web.
World Wide Web	A subset or cross-section of the Internet consisting of all the resources that can be reached by means of the HTTP protocol or any other Internet protocols that a Web browser can understand.

Table 1.1 World Wide Web Jargon *(continued)*

A TRIP AROUND THE BLOCK

Here's an example of a test drive with Netscape, the most widely distributed Web browser. Naturally, you have to start the program.

The program starts and connects to your default home page. At this point you could type in a Web address in the small address window, choose a site saved on your Bookmarks menu (more on bookmarks later in this chapter), or click a jumping-off point from this page (see Figure 1.1).

Sometimes you'll have to make a few jumps before getting to what you're interested in. Peppered throughout the Web are useful jumping-off places such as the Yahoo directory shown in Figure 1.2.

When you find your way to a destination on the Web, you'll still be able to jump elsewhere. Most Web sites contain links to other sites, in an effort to interconnect themselves. The most important button on any browser is the Back button (or the backward pointing arrow). It allows you to retrace your steps and follow other paths (see Figure 1.3).

So now I've followed a straight path (Welcome to Netscape | Exploring the Net | Internet Directory | Yahoo Directory | Photography | Magazine | Internet Photo Magazine Japan). Not only can I wander back and forth along that "history" path, I can also branch off at any point and pursue a new direction. This is the pleasure and the curse of the Web.

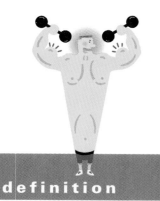

definition

history: The list of Web addresses you've visited during this session. It's called a Go list in some browsers and a path in general.

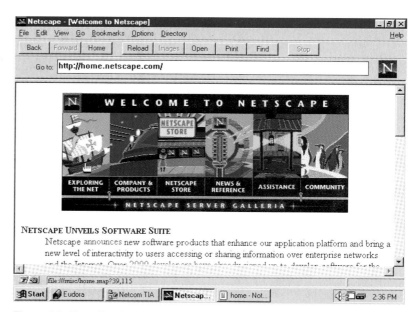

Figure 1.1 Here I'm clicking Exploring the Net on the Welcome to Netscape page. Next I'll click Internet Directory on the Exploring the Net page. The rest of this page features Netscape announcements—today mentioning the up-coming Netscape Navigator version 2.0 that will be out by the time this book goes to press.

Notice the News (Daily, Current Events, and so on) links on the Yahoo page. One of the great advantages of the Web as a publishing medium is its flexibility and ability to adapt to the latest current news.

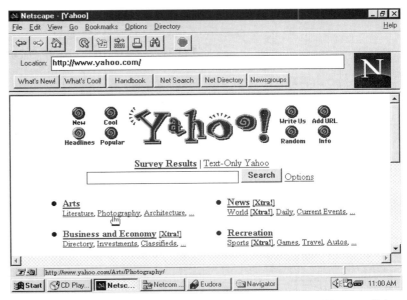

Figure 1.2 On the Internet Directory page I clicked the Yahoo Directory link to get here. Now I'm clicking the Photography link listed under Arts.

habits & strategies

When you arrive at the home page of a new site on the Web, or at any useful central jumping-off point ("node" in nerdspeak), make a bookmark there so you can find it, in the future, more easily.

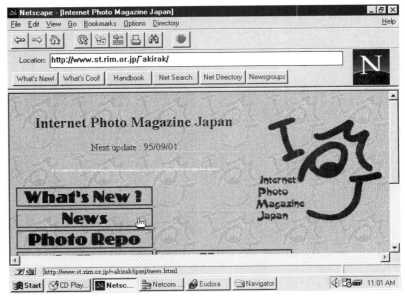

Figure 1.3 I clicked the Magazine link on the Photography page and then jumped here to *Internet Photo Magazine Japan* (in its URL, the .jp stands for Japan). I can now follow any single link from this home page and then jump back here to choose another link, as often as I like.

RETURN TO SENDER

The Internet is still a haphazard collection of networks and you won't always be able to make the connection you want. Sometimes, especially during peak hours (more or less the normal work week in the U.S.), your browser will fail to connect to the page you want. In general, all traffic on the Internet is highest during these times, and popular servers can slow down or even crash when "hit" by too many clients. Even sites that are available 24 hours a day, seven days a week, still need to shut down occasionally for maintenance or in the event of a crash.

You'll see an error message, perhaps alluding to something called a "failed DNS server look up" or what have you, but ignore that, as it's usually just a knee-jerk guess about what went wrong (usually a symptom of busy or overworked networks). Most of the time, all that happened was that some attempt to connect along the route "timed out"; that is, gave up before connecting successsfully.

Sometimes your browser won't acknowledge that it's hung up somewhere. Instead it will just keep churning away as if it's really loading up a page, but nothing new will happen, and the thermometer-like readout that shows the progress will stop growing. When your browser gives up, whether it admits it or not, press the Stop button and try again.

Another "problem" you may run into is not knowing the exact address of or any specific route to the information or site you want to reach. In that case, you'll want to use one of the many search mechanisms available on the Web. See Chapter 10 for more information on searching.

USING THE WEB WITHOUT WASTING TIME

The trickiest thing about making efficient use of the World Wide Web is that it's essentially a digressive medium, perfectly suited for long asides and fascinating tangents, less well suited for hard-core finite research.

There are two things you can do to spend your time on the Web more efficiently. The first is something I cannot emphasize strongly enough: make bookmarks. Make Bookmarks. *MAKE BOOKMARKS!* The Web is so peripatetic that you're bound to visit interesting sites,

CAUTION

With most browsers, once you back up and then head in a new direction, the branch you explored earlier will disappear from your path. Here again, it pays to make bookmarks.

habits & strategies

If any Web page takes over 90 seconds to load up, stop the browser and try again or come back later. You're too busy to sit there twiddling your thumbs while computers fail to connect with each other.

See Chapter 11 for how to download a bookmark-manager called SmartMarks from Netscape.

and then *never see them again*, because you won't remember exactly which tangents you followed to get there. You can always remove bookmarks that you end up not needing, so make a bookmark every time you arrive at an interesting-looking site. Later on, you'll be glad you did.

The other best advice I can offer is to separate out your business or educational usage of the Web from your recreational use. To save time on the Web, set yourself a goal and head for it as directly as you can. If, along the way, you are tempted by the siren call of interesting links, note them or make bookmarks for them, but leave them for another time.

THE REST OF THE BOOK

Well, there's more to this book than coverage of the World Wide Web. That's because, contrary to all the hype you may have heard recently, there's a lot more to the Internet than just the Web. In fact, the highest volume usage (discounting huge binary files, such as graphics) of the Internet is still (and probably always will be) electronic mail. Chapter 2 shows you the ropes for using specific Web browsers, but after that you'll plunge into the world of e-mail, mailing lists, discussion groups, and so on.

You don't have to read this book straight through. Pick the chapters that interest you. The whole book is thoroughly cross-referenced, so you won't miss anything (unless you want to). Whenever possible, I will include useful or informative Web addresses where you can get hands-on experience or find information about any given topic.

MAIL

Using Your
Web Browser

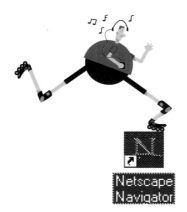

FAST FORWARD

START NETSCAPE ➤ *pp 20-21*
1. Click the Start button.
2. Point to Programs.
3. Select Netscape.
4. Double-click the Netscape Navigator icon in the Navigator folder.

START MS INTERNET EXPLORER ➤ *pp 37-38*
Double-click the Internet icon on your desktop.

FOLLOW A LINK ➤ *pp 25-26, 28-29*
(Links are called shortcuts in Internet Explorer.)
1. Move your mouse pointer to a highlighted word or illustration so that the pointer changes from an arrow to a hand.
2. Click the link.

GO BACK AND FORWARD ➤ *pp 26, 42*
• To go back, click the Back button in the toolbar.
• To go forward, click the Forward button in the toolbar.
• To go to a different point on your path:
In Netscape, select Go | *the name of the page.*
In Internet Explorer, select File | *the name of the page.*

CHOOSE A DIFFERENT HOME PAGE ➤ *pp 27, 42-43*

In Netscape follow these steps:
1. Select (or have handy) the exact wording of the Web address (you can go to the page and copy it from the Location window).
2. Select Options | Preferences.
3. Click the Styles tab.
4. Type or paste the address into the Home Page Location box.
5. Click OK.

In Internet Explorer follow these steps:
1. Go to the page you want to use as your home page.
2. Select View | Options.
3. Click the Start Page tab (Internet Explorer calls a home page a *start page*).
4. Click the Use Current button.
5. Click OK.

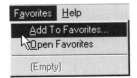

MAKE A BOOKMARK ➤ *pp 30, 42*
- In Netscape, select Bookmarks | Add Bookmark.
- In Internet Explorer, select Favorites | Add to Favorites. (Internet Explorer calls bookmarks *Favorites*.)

GO TO A BOOKMARK ➤ *pp 30, 42*
- In Netscape, select Bookmarks | *page name*.
- In Internet Explorer, select Favorites | *page name*.

PUT A SHORTCUT
TO A BROWSER ON YOUR DESKTOP ➤ *pp 45-46*

1. Open a folder containing the browser or a preexisting shortcut to it.
2. Click the icon for the browser.
3. Drag it onto the desktop.

PUT A BROWSER
ON YOUR START MENU ➤ *p 46*

1. Open a folder containing the browser or a preexisting shortcut to it (unless a shortcut already exists on the desktop).
2. Click the icon for the browser.
3. Drag it onto the Start button.

If Chapter 1 whetted your appetite to check out the World Wide Web for yourself, then it's time for you to fire up a Web browser and start exploring. There are quite a few browsers out there, many of which are variations on NCSA Mosaic, the original graphical Web browser. By far the most widely distributed browser is Netscape Navigator, usually just referred to as Netscape. By giving away early versions of the browser to individuals (it's still free to educational institutions, nonprofits, and others), Netscape established a dominant position in the browser market, so even competing browsers tend to offer the same features as Netscape.

The Windows 95 Plus! Pack Internet Jumpstart Kit includes Microsoft's entry in the browser market, the Internet Explorer. You can also obtain this browser from the Microsoft Network and elsewhere. The Internet Explorer is based on Mosaic but includes most of the capabilities of Netscape. Both Internet Explorer and Netscape versions 1.2 and later are Windows 95-savvy, capable of recognizing the desktop, handling long filenames, and creating shortcuts. I'll show you how to set up and use both of these browsers, because the odds are that you'll have access to at least one if not both of them. Even if you end up using some other browser, most of the features will be the same.

First, I'll give you a basic rundown on how to work with any browser. Then I'll show you how to use Netscape and Internet Explorer step by step.

WEB BROWSER BASICS

No matter what kind of Web browser or even what sort of Internet connection you have, the overall process of running a browser and connecting to the Web is more or less the same. Sometimes the terminology or the actual mechanism will vary from program to

CAUTION

If you don't have an Internet connection or don't know whether or not you are connected, see Appendix A.

*For graphical browsers, you'll
also want to know how to turn
off automatic picture loading.*

*Any time you change your mind
about going to a page, simply hit
the Stop button on your toolbar
(or press Escape). The page will
stop loading. You can also use
this technique to avoid connecting to your home page when you
start your browser, in order to
type an address in directly,
for example.*

program, and all browsers don't share the exact same set of capabilities, but the differences are getting smaller all the time.

With any Web browser, you'll need to know how to

- Start the program
- Navigate the Web by following links
- Type in a Web address to go to it directly
- Go to a bookmark
- Move backward and forward along your recent path
- Make a bookmark
- Assign a favorite Web page as your home page

Once you have these basic techniques down, browsing the Web is simply a matter of starting your program and then following links, visiting bookmarks, and entering addresses directly.

NETSCAPE—THE MOST POPULAR WEB BROWSER

For the near future, at the very least, Netscape appears to be the browser of destiny. According to some research, nearly three-quarters of the Web browsers out there are versions of Netscape. Suffice it to say that at some time or another you'll be using this browser, so it's probably a good one to start with.

Starting Netscape

To start Netscape, select Start | Programs | Netscape.

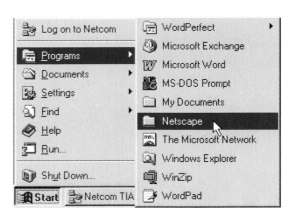

To get the latest version of Netscape (Navigator 2.0) either point any Web browser at the Netscape home page (http://home.netscape.com), click the Netscape Now! link and then follow the instructions; or (if, for example, you don't have an Internet connection or a Web browser of any kind set up), just go into any major computer software store and purchase a shrink-wrapped version of Netscape Navigator off the shelf.

This will open the Navigator folder. Double-click the Netscape Navigator shortcut icon.

(If this is the first time this version of Netscape has been run on your computer, a Netscape License Agreement dialog box will appear. Read the agreement and then click the Accept button.) Netscape will start up and will connect you to the Netscape home page, called Welcome to Netscape (see Figure 2.1).

Figure 2.1 The Welcome to Netscape page, featuring a clickable illustration to take you to many of the services linked from this page

Set It and Forget It

Take the time now to set up your copy of Netscape. If you're too busy to do it right now, make a point of coming back to this section later, when you have the time. Some of the instructions I'll give you later in this chapter won't work exactly the way I describe until you set up your copy of Netscape.

Hide the Directory Buttons

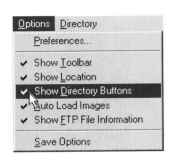

I've got nothing against the Directory buttons, per se, but they take up too much of your precious window. Each of the buttons corresponds to an option on the Directory menu, which has additional options to boot, so just use that menu.

To take the Directory buttons off the screen, select Options | Show Directory Buttons. The Directory buttons will disappear. Repeat to bring them back if you want.

Turn Off Link Underlining

I'm going out on a limb here, but I feel strongly about this: Web pages look much better without underlined words all over the screen. Links are already a different color from the rest of the text (usually blue vs. black), but the default underlining draws unnecessary emphasis to link words and destroys the typographical look of a Web page.

To turn off link underlining select Options | Preferences.

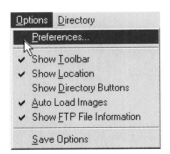

This brings up the Preferences dialog box. Click the Styles tab if it's not already in front (see Figure 2.2). While you're at it, decide if you want your toolbar buttons to appear as just Pictures (the default—not bad once you learn what each symbol means!), as just Text (my preference—they take up less space and you can read what each button does), or as both Pictures and Text. Click the "Links are" check box in the Link Styles area to uncheck Underlined.

Chapter 3 explains more about e-mail, and Chapter 6 covers Usenet news

Set Up Your Browser's E-mail Features

If you're lucky, someone will have installed Netscape for you and set up your e-mail information in it properly, and you won't have to do anything except verify it. More likely you'll at least have to enter your own personalizing information (such as your name). In the worst-case scenario, you'll also have to enter some of the technical e-mail address information. If so, I'll help you figure it out.

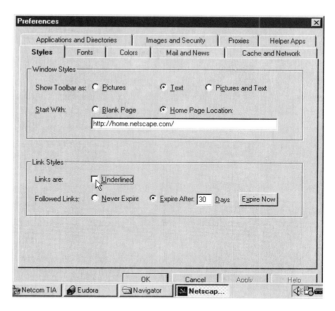

Figure 2.2 You'll be glad you turned off underlining, believe me.

In the Preferences dialog box (Options | Preferences), click the Mail and News tab (see Figure 2.3).

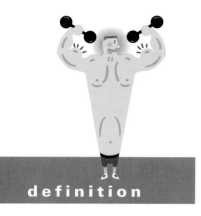

servers: The machines that handle the sorting and routing of your e-mail and news.

- Ignore the first box for now.
- Make sure the Your Name box show your correct name, the way you want it to appear on your outgoing e-mail.
- If you know your e-mail address, make sure it appears correctly in the Your Email box.
- If you know what a signature file is, have one on your PC, and want to see it attached to the end of your outgoing e-mail and Usenet posts, enter its path and filename in the Signature File box or click the Browser button, find the file, and click Open.

If the content of the Mail (SMTP) Server box at the top of the dialog box is just the word *mail*, or if that box or the News (NNTP) Server box are empty, then you'll have to get the addresses of your mail and Usenet news servers from your system administrator, and then type them in these boxes exactly.

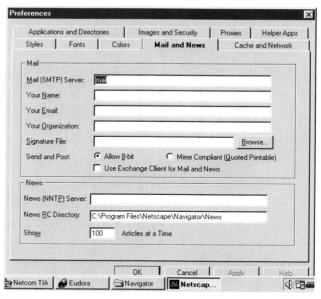

Figure 2.3 Ideally, someone else has filled in all this information for you already.

That's all you have to deal with. Click OK to keep your preferences. From now on, you can just run the program and forget about the setup.

Using Your Home Page as a Starting Point

When you start up your browser, it has to open somewhere. The lingo is that it starts off "pointing at" some address on the Web. Most browsers come configured to start you off on a page maintained by the maker of the browser. Some may come to you configured to start you off at your company's or department's home page on the Web.

Usually, the home page where you begin will have all kinds of useful starting places, for random Web "surfing," for specific information resources, and for search utilities that can lead almost anywhere on the Internet.

Netscape's Built-In Directory Links

Your browser may also have some useful links built into its menus or toolbars. Netscape's Directory menu has a plethora of useful starting places. Select Directory | Internet Directory to approach the Web from a top-down perspective.

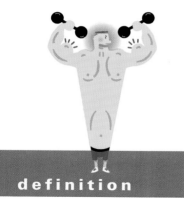

definition

home page: *1. The primary page of a Web site, the front door, the hub. 2. The page a Web browser automatically starts at. 3. An individual's personal page on the Web.*

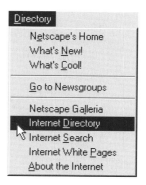

This takes you to Netscape's Internet Directory page, which mainly points to the infinitely more useful Yahoo directory. Yahoo is one of the most comprehensive categorical listings of Web pages.

Browsing by Following Links

Most of the time, you'll go from page to page on the Web by clicking hypertext links. These are highlighted words (or images) that, when clicked, jump you to another page or section of a page. Click the Yahoo Directory link (see Figure 2.4).

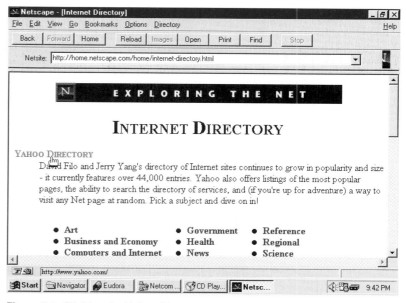

Figure 2.4 Clicking the Yahoo Directory link

You can also click one of the specific categories to go directly to that Yahoo subsection, but you might as well visit the main Yahoo page, especially this first time. At the Yahoo page, click the Literature link under Arts, the first item (see Figure 2.5). You'll be taken to the "Yahoo - Arts: Literature" page.

Going Back and Forward

Now suppose you change your mind (maybe after looking around this page a little) and would have liked to go elsewhere from the previous page. Or better yet, suppose you decide you'd like to make a bookmark of the main Yahoo page or even make that page into your home page? In any of these cases, you'll want to go "back" to the previous page. The command for this action in Netscape (and all other browsers I've ever encountered) is called Back.

Click the Back button on the toolbar to go back to the Yahoo home page.

SHORTCUT

You can also press ALT-LEFT ARROW or select GO| BACK to go backward to the previous page.

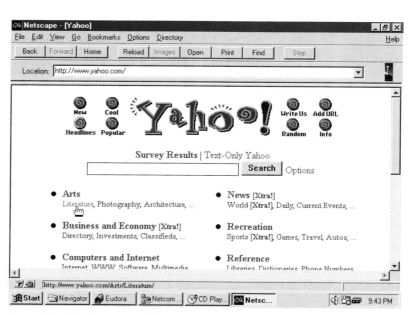

Figure 2.5 This is the main Yahoo page, a great jumping-off point. All of the links on this page lead to multitudes of other interesting links.

*If you encounter another page you'd
like to start using as your home page,
you can follow these same instructions
with that page.*

Making a Different Page
Your Home Page

Now suppose you did actually want to make the Yahoo page your
default home page (the one that would come up whenever you started
Netscape). You could do worse. Follow these steps to make the Yahoo
page your home page:

1. Click in the Location box and select the Web address of the
   page you're on.

2. Press CTRL-C to copy the address. Then select Options |
   Preferences and click the Styles tab. Click in the Start With
   box in the Window Styles area and press CTRL-V to paste the
   address into the box (see Figure 2.6).
3. Click OK.
4. Click the Forward button to return to the Arts:Literature page.

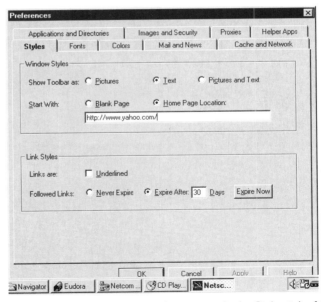

Figure 2.6 Make a different page your home page in the Styles tab of the
Preferences dialog box.

Browsing from Link to Link

Scroll through the page and click on the Literary E-zines link.

- Literary E-zines@ *(87)* NEW!
- Literature and Medicine (Medical Humanities)

This takes you to Yahoo's Entertainment:Magazines:Literary page (Yahoo is very well cross-referenced, so that pages of links are accessible under various categories). Click the link for *Enterzone*, a hypertext Web magazine (that I publish).

- Enterzone - writing, art, and new media featuring criticism, fiction, poetry, philosophy, hypertexts, computer graphics, interactive artforms, scanned photography, and drawings.

This takes you to the Enterzone home page, which changes every three months so the example will look different (see Figure 2.7). Clicking the first link on the page of Enterzone episode 3 takes me to a picture called Spring Gris Gris (see Figure 2.8).

Figure 2.7 The Enterzone home page. You've now entered a new sphere on the Web, a new home page. From this page there are all kinds of links both to parts of this specific site and to other destinations on the Web.

Figure 2.8 Spring Gris Gris (by Steve Seebol), which looks much better on a real computer screen. (It's at http://enterzone.berkeley.edu/ez/e3/articles/ seebol/springgrisgris.html if you want to jump there directly instead of hunting around for back issues.)

Going Back via the Go Menu

To jump back to a specific page earlier on your path, click the Go menu and choose the page directly. To get back to the Arts:Literature page, click the Go menu and select Yahoo - Arts:Literature.

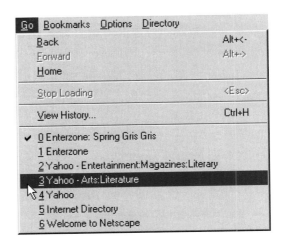

definition

bookmark: *A saved Web address that you can jump to instantly. Also called a hotlist entry, a Favorite, or SmartMark. (See Chapter 11 for more on SmartMarks.)*

habits & strategies

Normally, you have to go to a page before you can add a bookmark, but you can right-click on a link and choose "Add Bookmark for this Link" to add a link to your bookmarks without going to it.

Making a Bookmark

If you get to a page you find interesting, but you don't have the time to explore it and all of its links completely in one sitting, consider making a bookmark for that page. I recommend making bookmarks as often as possible. They're easy enough to get rid of, but it can be very hard to find your way back to a page you vaguely remember from an earlier Web session.

To make a bookmark for the current page, select Bookmarks | Add Bookmark.

The page will then appear at the bottom of the Bookmark menu next time you pull it down. Now choose a different link from the page you went back to (Arts:Literature). Click the Gutenberg EText World Wide link.

- **Fiction** *(48)* NEW!
- Freethought Web - Collection of freethought lit by such authors as Charles Bradlaugh, Joseph McCabe, Charles Watts, and Thomas Paine. Complete works of Robert G. Ingersoll
- Gutenberg EText World Wide
- **Institutes** *(6)*
- **Journals** *(8)*
- **Literary E-zines@** *(87)* NEW!

This takes you to the Project Gutenberg home page (see Figure 2.9). You can learn about Project Gutenberg or read or download any of their online texts from the Project Gutenberg home page.

Project Gutenberg's mission is to republish as much text as possible in electronic form and distribute it as freely as possible. To add this page to your bookmark list, select Bookmarks | Add Bookmark. (Notice that the previous bookmark you added is now on the list.)

SHORTCUT

Press CTRL-A to add the current

page to your bookmarks

Figure 2.9 The Gutenberg home page.

**habits &
strategies**

If a Web address starts with

http:// (as many do), you can

leave off that part of the address

when you type it in. By default,

Netscape will assume a URL

begins with it.

Entering Addresses Automatically

The one other way to visit a destination on the Web is to type in its address directly. If you are sent a Web address (a URL) in e-mail or some other onscreen medium, then you can select and copy the address and then paste it directly into Netscape's Location window. Otherwise, you'll have to click in the Location window (it will change its name to the Go To window). The current address will become selected. Type the new address directly over it. For example, type **http://www.emf.net/~mal** to visit a fascinating and always changing Web site.

You might notice that you're taken to one page and then immediately whisked off to another. With Netscape's latest browsers and certain pages, some actions will occur automatically, whether you select a link or not. If you're ever taken to some page you don't want to be at, just use your Back button or Go menu to head back to familiar territory.

Almost immediately, you'll appear at the main page of Malcolm's House of Vicarious Diversions (or something similar, the name changes frequently too), as shown in Figure 2.10.

Scroll down to the section called "some web projects I nurture" and select the Theremin link (see Figure 2.11). This takes you to a page about Leon Theremin, the inventor of an electronic musical instrument by the same name. (What a coincidence!)

Making a Shortcut

Windows 95 enables you to sequester shortcut icons all over your desktop and in folders to enable you to reach specific programs, documents, and folders directly. Similarly, Windows also recognizes Internet shortcuts that lead to sites on the Web. You can create such a shortcut icon at any time.

To do so, just right-click on some empty space in a Web page and choose Create shortcut from the menu that pops up (see Figure 2.12).

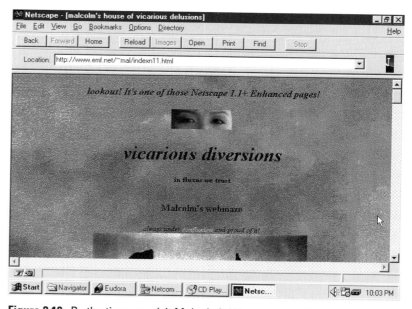

Figure 2.10 By the time you visit Malcolm's Web maze it will probably look somewhat different from this, since, unlike paper publications, Web sites can evolve daily.

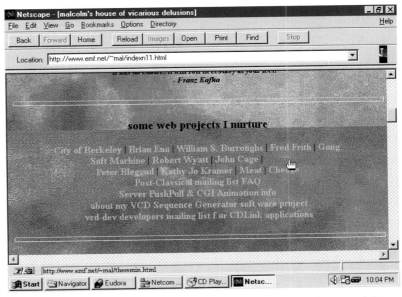

Figure 2.11 Most Web sites combine a certain amount of native material with links to other locations on the Web that the author of the site finds interesting.

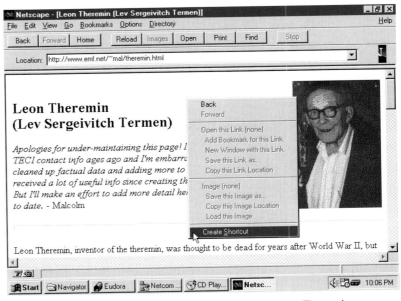

Figure 2.12 I'm making a shortcut to this page about Leon Theremin.

Netscape will suggest a name for the shortcut (based on the title of the Web page). Change the title if you want (perhaps to shorten it), and then click OK.

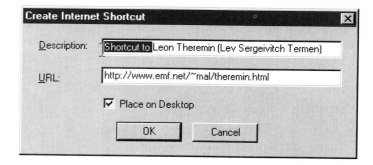

The shortcut will appear on your desktop. If the name is still too long, click on the label and then rename the icon.

You can save the text contents (as well as the embedded hypertext links) in the form of an .HTM (Web document source) file, in much the same way. Press CTRL+S or select File | Save as, and then save the document.

Saving an Image to Your Computer

netiquette

There's nothing wrong with saving other people's images on your computer. Just don't republish the art, on the Web or in another medium, without the expressed permission of the artist and original publisher.

If you see an image on a Web page that you'd like to save on your own computer, you can snatch it easily with Netscape. Just right-click on the image you want to save and choose "Save this Image as...".

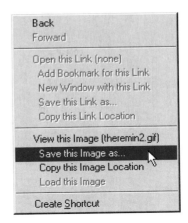

See Chapter 3 for an explanation of Internet e-mail. See Chapter 6 for more on Usenet news and posting articles.

A Save As dialog box will appear. Change the name if you want, or where the image will be saved, and then click the Save button.

Sending E-mail from the Web

There are two ways to send e-mail while Web browsing, but each of them uses the exact same mechanism in Netscape. Some Web pages have e-mail links, also referred to as *mailto* links (because the name of the protocol for the URL of such a link is mailto, as in mailto:xian@pobox.com). Click on one of these links, and Netscape will open up a mail dialog box with the e-mail of the recipient automatically in place, drawn from the link URL. These links allow Web publishers to invite easy interaction from the audience.

But you don't need a mailto link to send e-mail from within Netscape. You can also select File | Mail Document. This brings up a Send Mail/Post News dialog box (see Figure 2.13). Netscape suggests a Subject (the title of the page), and pastes the current URL into the first line of the message window.

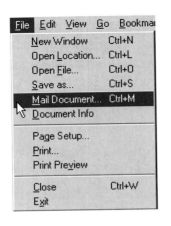

To send e-mail from the Web follow these steps:

1. Type an e-mail address in the Mail To box.
2. Write your message.
3. To include the text of the current Web page in your e-mail message, click the Quote Document button in the bottom center of the dialog box.
4. Click the Send button when you're done.

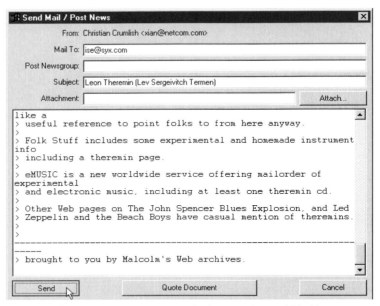

Figure 2.13 Send e-mail to anyone on the Internet from within Netscape, and include the text contents of your current Web page, if you like.

Printing a Web Page

Even though most people read Web pages online, jumping from page to page like a TV-watcher skirting advertisements, you can easily print out an interesting page to read at your leisure or to send to someone who lacks Internet access. Just select File | Print and then click OK. If you want to preview the page, select File | Print Preview. This changes Netscape to a Print Preview mode similar to that of a word-processing program (see Figure 2.14).

Click the magnifying glass icon anywhere to zoom in to that place. Repeat to zoom in closer and, after three clicks, back out again. If everything looks OK, click the Print button.

Quitting Netscape

When you're finished browsing, and have made bookmarks to all the tantalizing loose ends that you plan to pursue later, quit Netscape by selecting File | Exit (or clicking the Close button in the upper-right corner of your screen). Then, perhaps, close the Navigator window. And get back to work!

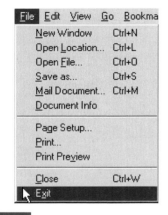

habits & strategies

If the document looks like it will take up too many pages, change to a smaller font size and try again.

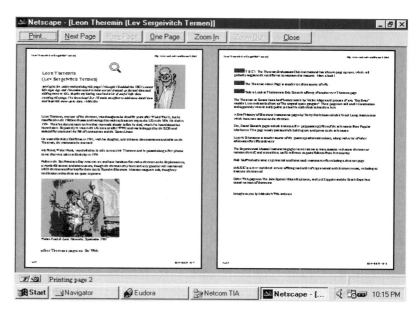

Figure 2.14 You can preview a Web page before printing it.

CAUTION

Don't confuse Internet Explorer with Windows Explorer, the Windows 95 program that shows you a tree view of your folders and files.

THE MICROSOFT WEB BROWSER

If you've installed the Microsoft Plus! Pack with its Internet Jumpstart Kit, or joined the Microsoft Network with full Internet access, or obtained a copy of Microsoft Internet Explorer in any other way, then you have a browser that's very similar to Netscape, and at least as well integrated into the Windows 95 operating system.

Windows 95 Terminology

Partly as a consequence of Internet Explorer's compliance to Windows 95 standards, some of the terminology you'll encounter using IE (as I'll call it from now on) differs from the words used by everyone else on the Internet. To save yourself from embarrassing *faux pas* in front of Internet purists, Table 2.1 provides you with some translations.

Depending on which Web browser was installed most recently on your computer, double-clicking on the Internet shortcut icon will either start up the Internet Explorer or some other browser aimed at the Web address the shortcut points to.

What Everyone Else on the Web Calls	Microsoft Calls
A link	A shortcut
A home page	A start page
Bookmarks (or hotlist)	Favorites
Images	Pictures
Reloading a page	Refreshing

Table 2.1 Translating between Internet jargon and Microsoft-speak

Starting Internet Explorer

Internet Explorer creates on your desktop an icon called the Internet (somewhat presumptuously), so to start Internet Explorer, just double-click that icon.

Internet Explorer starts you at a page called Microsoft Welcomes You To The Internet! (see Figure 2.15). This page may change, and, as with any browser, you can assign a different page as your home page (or start page).

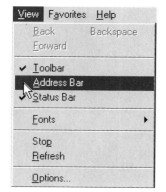

Set It and Forget It

As with any browser, you should take the time now to set up a few things so that you can forget about the setup from now on. First of all, you'll want to be able to see what Web address you're viewing (and be able to enter new addresses conveniently in the same space). So select View | Address Bar.

The Address bar appears. Then select View | Options.

The Options dialog box appears (see Figure 2.16).

Click the Underline Shortcuts check box in the Shortcuts area to turn off link underlining. (See the "Turn Off Link Underlining" section earlier in this chapter for my explanation of why link underlining is a Bad Thing.) Then click OK.

Figure 2.15 Microsoft's Internet Explorer home page.

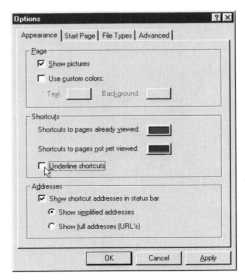

Figure 2.16 Turn off link underlining and do some other basic setup in the Options dialog box

Following Shortcuts

As with any Web browser, to explore a link (or shortcut, as Microsoft calls them), move your mouse pointer over the link so that the pointer changes into a hand and click. Click the main image in the middle of the Microsoft home page to set off onto the Internet. It will take you to the Explore the Internet page (see Figure 2.17).

This starting page is fine if you want to learn all about Microsoft and its wonderful products and good works in general. If not, as with any mega-corporate page, look for the "interesting links" section and start surfing. Click the Links to other sites "shortcut" on the Explore the Internet page. Then click the News link on the Cool Links page that comes up. This takes you to the Cools Links: News page, where you can find some newspapers and other news services as well as links to the ubiquitous Yahoo directory (see Figure 2.18).

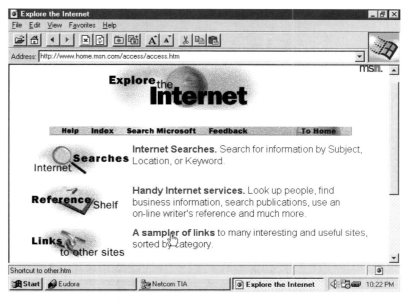

Figure 2.17 Explore some of the links to other sites from the Microsoft home page.

Figure 2.18 Microsoft's Cool Links: News should send you to some good perusing spots to accompany your morning coffee.

Go Back and Forward

The easiest ways to retrace your steps back along the path you've taken and then forward again down a path you just explored is to click the Back and Forward buttons on the toolbar. Try it now. Click the Back button.

Then click the Forward button.

Favorite Places

To be consistent with other Windows 95 programs—which all look to the same folder (C:\Windows\Favorites) for shortcuts to your most common folders and documents—the Internet Explorer saves shortcuts to your favorite Web pages in this same place. Instead of adding a bookmark to your hotlist, as various other Web browsers refer to it, you add a page to your Favorites, but the idea is the same.

To add a page (such as the Yahoo news page called News from Reuters Online) to your Favorites, select Favorites | Add To Favorites.

A dialog box called Add to Favorites that looks like a standard Save As dialog box appears. Change the name for the shortcut if you like and then click the Add button. The page will then appear on the Favorites menu as well as in the Favorites folder. (Select Favorites | Open Favorites to see the contents of that folder.)

MAKING A NEW PAGE YOUR START PAGE

If you decide you'd like to have Internet Explorer start you off somewhere else automatically (such as at the main Yahoo page), first go to that page. Then do the following:

1. Select View | Options.
2. Click the Start Page tab in the Options dialog box.
3. Then click the Use Current button (see Figure 2.19).
4. Then click OK.

SHORTCUT

Internet Explorer also keeps track of all the pages you've been to this session on its File menu (at the bottom, in the same place that a word processor lists recently opened documents). This makes it easy to jump back to a page you visited earlier in the session.

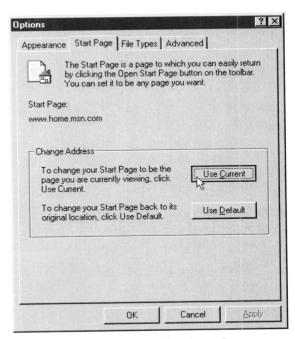

Figure 2.19 Make the current page your "start page".

If you ever want to return to the Microsoft home page, type the address **www.home.msn.com** into the Address window (as explained in the next section). To revert to the original start page, click the Use Default button in the Start Page tab of the Options dialog box.

Entering Addresses

To go directly to a specific Web address, type (or paste) the exact address into the Address Bar window just below the toolbar and press ENTER. Say someone has told you about the Internet Underground Music Archive and sent you the Web address. You'd just paste or type **http://www.iuma.com** into the Address window (the name of the box changes to Open when you enter the text), and press ENTER.

IUMA's Welcome to IUMA page appears. You realize that there's a world of stuff here that you'd like to explore but you're much too busy to check it out right now, so add the page to your Favorite places (Figure 2.20).

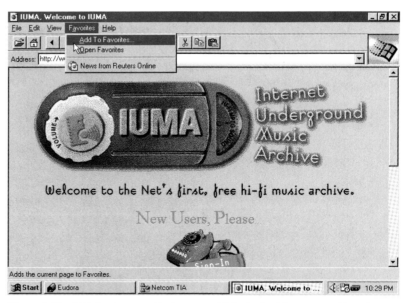

Figure 2.20 Add the Internet Underground Music Archive to your Favorites (if you like music).

Making a Shortcut

To make a shortcut to the current page, select File | Create Shortcut, or right-click in some free space on the page and choose Create Shortcut from the menu that pops up.

Internet Explorer will place the shortcut on your desktop.

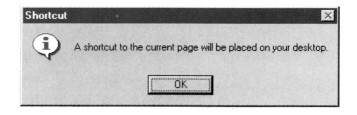

For more on specific e-mail programs, see Chapter 4.

E-mail with Internet Explorer

If you click on a mail to link (shortcut) in Internet Explorer, it will automatically launch whichever e-mail program you have integrated into your operating system and your local network (if any). This could be Microsoft Exchange or just about any other mail program that can handle Windows' MAPI standards (which neither of us want to get into, right?).

You can drag Internet shortcuts into an e-mail message window, at least with Exchange, and send the shortcut to anyone else using Windows 95. That person can simply double-click in her message window to launch a Web browser and visit the page you're promoting.

USING ANOTHER BROWSER

As I mentioned before, there are many different browsers out there. If you've got one besides the two I've explained, I think you'll be able to follow along, taking into account that some commands might appear on different menus or with slightly different names, and that shortcuts, long filenames, and other Windows 95 special features might not be supported.

PUTTING A BROWSER
ON THE DESKTOP

To create easy access to whichever browser you plan to use most of the time, you can drag a shortcut icon onto the desktop. Open the folder containing the browser (or a shortcut to it), and drag that icon onto the desktop. If Windows asks, make sure the icon created is a shortcut and not the original or a copy.

You can do this for Netscape by dragging the shortcut icon from the Navigator window, as shown here:

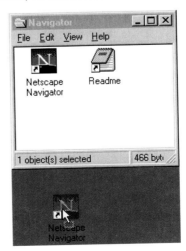

The Internet Explorer, of course, already has an icon on the desktop, thanks to Microsoft's foresight. You can drag an Internet shortcut icon (one that points to a Web page) onto a browser shortcut icon to launch the browser and aim it at the Web page all at once.

PUTTING A BROWSER ON THE START MENU

To add a browser to your Start menu, simply drag its program icon (or any shortcut to it) onto the Start button itself.

You can also drag the Internet icon from the desktop to make Internet Explorer available on the Start menu.

Then to run any browser, just click the Start button and choose it from the items at the top of the menu.

KEEPING UP WITH THE WEB

There's really no way you ever can keep up with the Web. It's changing and evolving so rapidly I'm not sure it even makes sense to talk about "keeping up" with it. However, there are a few things you can do to stay "in the loop."

One thing I'd recommend is subscribing to *Netsurfer Digest*. To check it out, visit its home page at http://www.netsurf.com/nsd/ (see Figure 2.21). Read the latest issue and see if you'd like to receive it. It comes more or less weekly and is sent as an e-mail message. You can save the message as an .HTM file and then load it into your Web browser (double-click it) to read the latest issue and follow any of the interesting links in the articles.

Another approach is to occasionally read the What's New or What's Cool pages at any of the major central pages you might encounter or start at, such as Netscape, Yahoo, NCSA, and so on. There are also several variations on the Cool Site of the Day concept out there

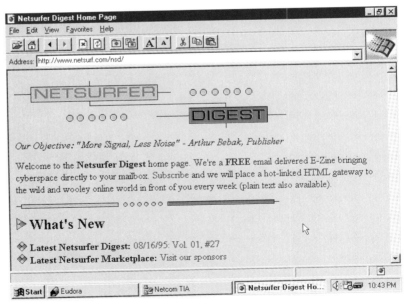

Figure 2.21 The *Netsurfer Digest* home page

(as well as links that fling you toward randomly selected pages, if you're really up for an adventure). For example, visit http://cool.infi.net (see Figure 2.22).

PUBLISHING ON THE WEB

Putting up your own pages on the Web is easier than you might think. See Chapter 12 for the lowdown.

INTERACTING ON THE INTERNET

Perhaps the biggest drawback of the Web, or at least of most of its contents, is that it places the user in a passive role. For all its possibilities, at this point using the Web isn't too far removed from watching television. The Internet did not grow in popularity this quickly simply as a venue for personal listings and corporate advertisements.

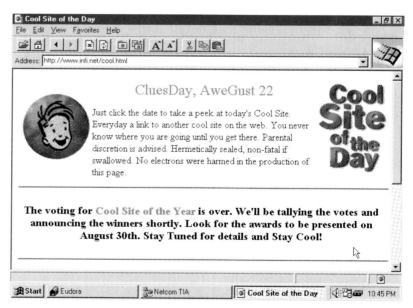

Figure 2.22 If you can get past the sophomoric verbiage, the Cool Site of the Day can keep you abreast of interesting new sites on the Web.

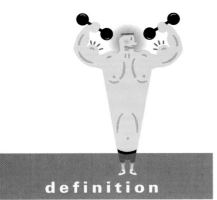

definition

IRC: Internet Relay Chat, a system for real-time (typed) conversation, explained in Chapter 8.

No, much of the culture of the Internet takes place in more interactive formats, such as in private e-mail, on semi-public mailing lists, and on the massive Usenet newsgroup system. Those craving live interaction find their way to the IRC or other "chat" venues.

There are already many experiments that incorporate these more interactive features into the Web experience, and if and when they become widespread or popular, the Web will absorb yet another aspect of the Internet. For now, though, you should poke your head beyond the Web browser and learn a little about e-mail and discussion groups, explained in the next six chapters.

FINDING INFORMATION

The other major activity on the Internet (besides communication) is research and the transferring of files. The Internet has made it easy for you to find answers to questions and to transfer informational files and fully functional programs directly to your computer. Many of these research and file-transferring activities can be pursued through your Web browser, but some specialized activities work best with programs designed for them. Both these specialized programs and Web techniques for searching and transferring files are explained in Chapter 9 and 10.

DON'T LET ME HOLD YOU BACK

The best service I can render you in this book is to offer a grounding in what's going on on the Internet and to show you how to work the controls of your browser and other software. After that, you've got an entire globe full of information and ideas to explore. I'll point you down some likely pathways, but mainly I'm going to get out of your way and let your natural interests draw you toward your own destinations. Welcome to the Internet.

E-Mail:
You Have New Mail

FAST FORWARD

SEND INTERNET E-MAIL ➤ *pp 56-57*

- If you're on a network, make sure there's an Internet e-mail gateway.
- Enter your recipient's e-mail address in the standard Internet format:
  their-username@their.Internet.address.

KEEP E-MAIL FROM TAKING OVER YOUR DAY ➤ *p 57*

Just check your messages a few times a day, instead of staying connected all the time and checking your messages compulsively. (This is one of those "do as I say, not as I do" rules.)

A TYPICAL E-MAIL SESSION ➤ *pp 57-58*

1. Run your mail program. It will tell you if you have new mail.
2. Select and read mail in your inbox.
3. Reply to a message, quoting from the original if necessary.
4. Send (or add to your queue) new mail (this is sometimes the first thing you'll do).
5. Quit your mail program.

I find you and your entire
family completely offensive. :-)

WHEN ON THE NET,
DO AS THE NETTERS DO ➤ *pp 58-62*
- When replying to e-mail, quote the salient part of the original message.
- Create a short signature to be attached to each message.
- When not in formal business situations, keep your e-mail tone conversational.
- If you are afraid someone might misinterpret what you say, consider appending a sideways smiley face. :-)

KEEP TRACK OF OTHERS'
E-MAIL ADDRESSES ➤ *p 62*
- Save e-mail messages from people as a quick-and-dirty way to store their addresses.
- Create "aliases" or "nicknames" for e-mail addresses you use often.
- Set up an address book with names and e-mail addresses.

Here's a shortcut to a Web page you might find

--xian

Leon Theremin

ATTACH A FILE TO AN E-MAIL MESSAGE ➤ *pp 62-63*
How you do this varies from network to network. It is still difficult to do this consistently across the Internet.

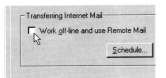

READ YOUR MAIL OFF-LINE ➤ *p 63*

To minimize your connect time, consider running an off-line mail program that will let you send and receive your messages all in a batch.

MARK AN URGENT
MESSAGE AS HIGH PRIORITY ➤ *p 64*

With most e-mail programs, you can assign a priority (up to "highest") to any message, if you want to get your recipient's attention.

PREPARE FOR A VACATION ➤ *pp 64-65*

1. Set up an outgoing vacation message so people will know why you're not responding to your mail.
2. Temporarily unsubscribe from high-traffic mailing lists.

```
I will be away from my e-mail for the next
respond to your mail about "Leon Theremin"

Aloha.

        --xian
```

One thing to watch out for is that the act of checking your e-mail can easily become addictive and destroy productivity. Be conscious of how you integrate the use of e-mail into your work (or even home) life, so it doesn't eat up more than its share of your time.

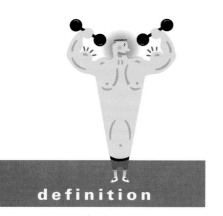

definition

asynchronous: A geek expression meaning "not happening at the same time."

When you get past the hype (and truly exciting developments) of the World Wide Web, you'll notice that what really holds the Internet together is e-mail. In a century that has seen the invention and widespread acceptance of the telephone and television, perhaps we've gotten all too accommodating of each new communication medium. In some ways, though, I'm surprised that the academics, researchers, and military that first populated the Internet managed to keep such as useful tool a secret for so long.

Probably the biggest advantage of e-mail as a form of communication is that it is *not* immediate. Sure, e-mail travels much more quickly than traditional paper mail (called "snail mail" by e-mailers), but, unlike a phone call, an e-mail message cannot demand immediate response. So e-mail enables you to "schedule" some of your communication with others and postpone interruptions until you're ready to attend to them.

Unlike voice mail, which is similarly asynchronous, e-mail enables you to keep a written correspondence. Still, you can't yet assume that your e-mail correspondents will necessarily see and respond to your mail in a timely fashion, so for urgent business matters it's best to employ additional means of communication.

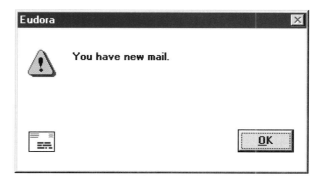

Compared to other forms of written communication (conventional mail, fax, telex, and so on), e-mail is also relatively cheap. Still, there's something tangibly more "likeable" about e-mail, compared with other forms of quick communication. Receiving written messages carries some (if not all) of the appeal of finding letters in your "real" mailbox. And unlike phone conversations, you can make sure you've said precisely what you wanted to say in exactly the right tone before pressing that "send" button. But I don't need to convince you about e-mail. If you're reading this book, the wave has already caught up with you and you're already on the Net.

In this chapter, I'll give you an overview of e-mail, so you understand the general procedures and terminology. In Chapter 4, I'll give you hands-on instructions for a couple of typical e-mail programs.

INTERNET MAIL VS. E-MAIL IN GENERAL

The Internet provides a common medium through which many different types of e-mail can be shared. It doesn't matter if you use Quickmail in your office and the person you want to send mail to is on America Online. With Internet mail addresses, you can send a message to that person just as if you were both on the same network. It only requires that the messages be formatted the same way with certain standard headers, which your e-mail program will take care of for you. Ideally, it will hide most of those headers from you as well.

Internet e-mail is a "plain text" medium, so don't expect your clever use of fonts, boldface, and graphic lines to go over well with your net-correspondents. It may go across a LAN to an office buddy just fine, but it will not make it through the eye of the needle that is an Internet mail gateway. For that matter, the methods for attaching files to e-mail messages are severely limited for mail that has to make it across the Internet before reachings its destination.

To some people, e-mail *is* the Internet, and e-mail traffic, after Web transactions, still represents the lion's share of Internet activity. Some people distinguish between the larger group of people who can send or receive Internet mail (referring to them as "on the Net") and the smaller but still large group of people who have direct connections to the Internet ("on the Internet").

However you look at it, an Internet e-mail address always appears in this form: *username@Internet-address*. The Internet-address portion takes the form *host.subdomain.domain*, with the host name sometimes

CAUTION

Some online services, such as CompuServe, charge for e-mail received, usually with a certain amount free; and many forms of Internet connectivity charge for connect time.

The reason you sometimes get e-mail with enormous headers is that the message originated in a different e-mail program.

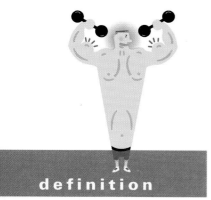

gateway: A program or computer that regulates communication between two networks, the Internet and a local network, or any two network media.

Tempting as it might be, don't keep your e-mail program running and connected all day long. Try to limit yourself to checking your mail two or three times a day (or even once a day, if you have Herculean self-control), perhaps at the beginning, middle, and end of your work day.

optional. To send e-mail to someone via the Internet, make sure their address takes this form. Generally, e-mail addresses are not case-sensitive (meaning they don't distinguish between uppercase and lowercase), and at worst, only the username can be.

E-MAIL FOR BUSY PEOPLE

When you are really busy, e-mail can be either a blessing or a curse (or both at the same time). Not having to drop what you're doing to reply to a query can help you organize your own time effectively. But don't let it interrupt you! If you're constantly checking your mail and getting involved in more and more casual online conversations, your productivity might suffer and e-mail can become another black hole eating up all your free time.

I don't want to make e-mail sound like a drag, though. Most people really enjoy it as a form of communication—just keep it within reasonable boundaries as part of your workday.

A TYPICAL MAIL SESSION

In Chapter 4, I'll explain the details of two very popular e-mail programs and give you enough to go on to use any program to read your mail. Here I'll just cover the outline of a generic mail session.

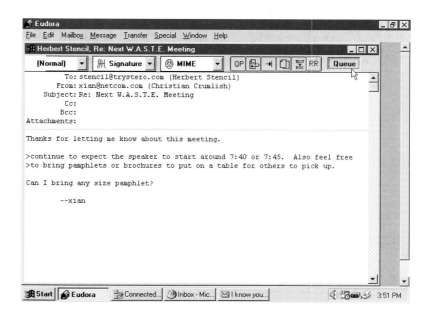

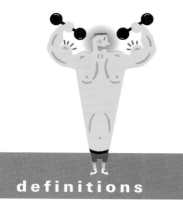

definitions

host: *The name of a specific machine in a larger domain or subdomain (such as squinky.microsoft.com), but you don't need to know any of this, really.*

domains and subdomains:

Ways of organizing Internet addresses. Domains are large areas divided by purpose (.com for commercial, .edu for education, etc.) and subdomains are smaller areas within those larger domains (ibm.com, harvard.edu).

1. Run your mail program. It will tell you if you have new mail.
2. Select and read mail in your inbox.
3. Reply to (or forward) messages, quoting from the original if necessary.
4. Save messages you'll need to deal with later and delete as much mail as you can.
5. Send new mail (this is sometimes the first thing you'll do).
6. Deal with older saved mail, if the time is ripe.
7. Quit your mail program.

SOME E-MAIL CONVENTIONS

As a new communication medium, e-mail has developed its own conventions. It's often easy to spot first-time e-mailers, because they tend to borrow from other familiar written styles. An e-mail message is not a postcard, not a letter, not an office memo (but can be similar to all three, naturally).

The headers in an e-mail message (To:, Date:, Subject:, and so on, some of which are filled out for you) make it resemble a memo, but most people write e-mail in a more informal style, reminiscent of conversation.

In the next few sections I'll describe some of the conventions of e-mail communication, so you can get into the swing of things as quickly as possible.

Quoting

It is common to quote some of the message you are responding to in a reply, to provide some context to your message. This is not always necessary, but as soon as you get a message from someone reading "I'm afraid not" or "Yes, let's do it!" and you can't remember what you said in your original message, you'll understand how helpful it is to include some of the original message in a reply.

```
When you wrote:

>If we upsnarch the quince-wimble, I think we'll have the problem under
>control.

I wasn't sure what you meant by "we."

    --xian
```

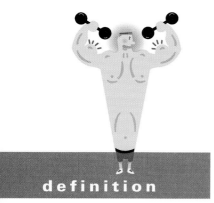

inbox: *The folder in your mail program that contains incoming mail, before it's been deleted or moved to another folder for storage.*

Most mail programs will automatically include the original message (or offer to do so) when you start to reply. Be sure to trim as much of the quotation as you can to save your recipient time rereading and to make sure that your reply doesn't get lost in the shuffle. Leave just enough of the original message to provide context. Also, use blank lines (press ENTER) between quoted text and new text so it doesn't all clump together.

If you're sending an unrelated message, delete all the quoted text. Change the Subject, too, while you're at it.

By the way, the system of quoting using greater than signs (>) or other characters in front of each line comes from UNIX mail programs, which until now have dominated Internet e-mail. Some programs change the color, font, and so on to show quotation but you can't assume that such enhancements will come across correctly on the Internet (as opposed to within your office), where the only common denominator is essentially the standard keyboard characters.

Sending Copies of E-Mail

To send e-mail to more than one recipient, you can either put the e-mail addresses all in the To: header of the new message, separated by commas (or, in some mail programs, by other characters such as semicolons), or you can enter additional addresses on the Cc: line (Cc originally stood for carbon copy, and has been rationalized since the demise of carbon as meaning courtesy copy). Addresses on the Cc line will receive a copy of the mail and will appear in the headers of the message, as seen by recipients.

Some e-mail programs also permit the use of a Bcc: line (standing for blind "carbon" copy). Addresses in the Bcc: header will receive a copy of the mail but will not appear in the message headers as seen by recipients.

Not all mail setups recognize the Bcc: header, so it does not provide perfectly reliable anonymity for your "blind" recipients.

Signatures

You may notice that all the mail you get from a correspondent ends with the same tag line, or even several lines. Usually, the person isn't typing that information into the end of each message but instead has something called a signature file that their mail program automatically

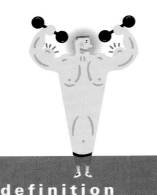

appends to each outgoing message. The text itself in a signature file is usually referred to as a signature, but signatures are also called sig blocks, sigs, .signatures, and .sigs (the latter two are UNIX terms), depending on whom you ask.

So what should you have in *your* signature, assuming you want one? Well, you'll at least want to include your name, and possibly your e-mail address (in case your recipient can't get it from the message automatically), but probably not your phone number. Some people include favorite or inane sayings, or elaborate drawings made of keyboard characters (called ASCII art after the name of the standard computer character set—ASCII).

```
            Hubert J. Wapshoe
            "Founder of the Internet"
```

Assuming you use e-mail for work, keep your signature business-like. Remember that once you've sent e-mail to anyone, there's a scrap of text with your name attached floating around, and you never know who it might get sent to or where you might end up seeing yourself quoted.

For personal correspondence, no one should resend your mail elsewhere without your permission, but it does happen.

Some programs vary or allow you to customize the quotation characters, frequently using a vertical bar (|), colon (:), or even the initials of the person being quoted. If you can customize your program, strive for readability.

habits & strategies

Keep your inbox under control by ruthlessly deleting obsolete mail and filing other messages in folders.

There are measures you can take to keep your e-mail more secure and private, some of which I'll touch on in Chapter 4.

Informality

Do not be offended if you receive mail that dispenses with the customary (in letters) Dear Sir-type salutation. Although many people will preface a message with "Hi," or anything from "Dear Ms. Higgenbotham" to "Hey Now!" it is completely acceptable to just plunge directly into a message, in that breathless, late-twentieth-century way.

Some e-mail correspondences resemble long, drawn-out (and thought-out) conversations, and written conversations also provide the potential for wordplay, visual puns, even collaborative poems, and so on. So slip off your shoes and relax before beginning your correspondence.

Smileys :-)

Of course by now you know about smileys, those sideways faces made from punctuation characters that are also sometimes called *emoticons*. Because e-mail is said to be a cold medium—conversational, yet lacking the facial, voice, and body language cues that people use in real life to smooth along interaction, there is a great danger of misinterpretation, of people taking offense, of erupting arguments.

You may have heard of the practice of "flaming," which essentially means chewing someone out in e-mail or in a discussion group, usually in an vitriolic and sometimes deliberately humorous (in a burlesque sense) sort of way. Such scurrilous attack mail is referred to as "flames." Many flames are provoked through the sort of ambiguity and offense-taking that I just alluded to. Thus the practice arose of appending a smiley, such as the basic one (tilt your head to the left),

```
:-)
```

to the end of anything even mildly controversial. (Certain popular abbreviations, such as IMHO (in my humble opinion) also aim for the same effect.) From there arose an entire vocabulary of smiley faces, many of them silly and rarely used. Semicolons are often substituted for colons to denote winking

```
;-)
```

and the "mouth" character can be changed to indicate frowning, or other less clear expressions.

```
>:-(
```

habits & strategies

It's still a good idea to maintain decorum in business correspondence.

Microsoft Exchange and other MS programs can all share an address book, as explained in Chapter 4.

There are whole books just on this minor semaphore-like communication form and I encourage you to pick one up if you are really interested (and apparently not too busy).

```
I find you and your entire family completely offensive. :-)
```

KEEPING TRACK OF OTHER PEOPLE'S ADDRESSES

Once you get online you'll need to start a collection of other people's e-mail addresses. Different e-mail programs have different ways of helping you deal with this. Most allow you to create something called an address book or a collection of "nicknames" or "aliases" that represent full e-mail addresses.

People are more and more including their e-mail addresses on business cards (some are even putting Web addresses there as well).

SOME E-MAIL EXTRAS

Internet e-mail standards are constantly evolving. Here are some of the features you'll want to use that are not yet widely implemented but getting there.

Attachments

Probably the biggest frustration with e-mail these days is sending files as attachments. This is no problem within a given network or within an online service such as AOL or CompuServe, but the methods used to attach files to Internet e-mail are not yet "spoken" by every type of mail gateway. You may have to inquire with your recipient (or sender) and possibly tech support as well to learn what specifically will or won't work. Even if you can send and receive attachments, you'll still have to agree on file formats that both you and your correspondent can work with.

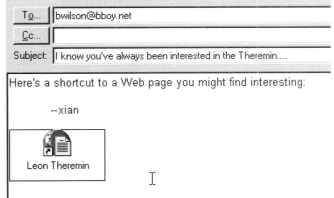

Here's a shortcut to a Web page you might find interesting:

--xian

Leon Theremin

Off-Line Mail Reading

Because some forms of Internet connectivity charge you the whole time you're connected, you might want to investigate handling your mail off-line. This means connecting briefly to download new mail and then disconnecting. You read your mail and compose your replies without being connected, and then connect again briefly to reply.

Not all mail readers or Internet accounts can do this, but the most popular ones can.

CAUTION

Some people (and entire Usenet newsgroups, such as alt.folklore.urban—see Chapter 6) abhor the use of smileys and will flame you mercilessly just for using them. Also, keep them out of for-the-record communication.

habits & strategies

If you need to exchange e-mail addresses with someone who does not remember their address, just ask them to send you mail (give them your address), and then you'll have captured their address in that first message.

netiquette

Even if you have flat-rate Internet access, it's still kinder to the network resources to connect occasionally, and send and receive all your mail at once, than to stay connected constantly and tie up modem lines, encouraging others to hog the lines as well rather than risk busy signals.

Prioritizing Mail

Most mail programs can assign a priority level to messages from highest, through normal, to lowest, to help a recipient realize that a message is urgent and requires a quick reply. Use this kind of signaling only when necessary or people will start to assume you're always crying wolf. In crises, though, a priority flag can really help a message stand out in a crowded inbox.

Filtering and Forwarding Mail Automatically

The future of e-mail is intelligent agents that filter and sort incoming mail, perhaps find information for you out on the Net, and even reply automatically to certain messages. For now, with some e-mail programs, you can set up automatic filtering or forwarding. Filtering means filing (or deleting) incoming messages based on key words found in the headers or contents of messages. Forwarding means automatically sending some or all of your mail to another address. (The term "to forward" is also applied to the manual task of sending an individual piece of mail on to another address.)

Receipt Confirmation

Some e-mail programs allow you to require that you be notified when your recipient has received (or even opened) your mail message. This trick isn't supported everywhere on the Net so for now it only works within specific networks.

Going on Vacation: The Overflowing Inbox

If you are going to be away from your mail for a while, you might want to set up an automatic vacation message to go out to anyone who mails you while you're gone. You do this so no one thinks you're blowing them off.

```
I will be away from my mail for the next two weeks (until July 29). I will reply
to your message about "Leon Theremin" when I return.

Aloha!

        --xian
```

If you subscribe to any very busy mailing lists (mailing lists are explained in Chapter 5), you might want to temporarily unsubscribe to avoid a deluge of mail on your return.

WHAT TO DO ABOUT UNSOLICITED MAIL

As e-mail becomes a ubiquitous medium, unsolicited e-mail messages, chain letters, and come-ons might start appearing in your mail box more and more often, just as unsolicited fax messages have started appearing. While this might not cost you money (unless your service provider charges you for mail), it is still a waste of your time as well as rude.

If you receive an unprompted message, send a reply to the sender asking where they got your address, and telling them not to send you any more mail (and to take you off any mailing list they may have put you on without asking). Also, if it continues to be a problem, send a Cc: copy of the message to postmaster@*their address* (use the same details after the @ sign in their address), so they know you mean business and so their mail administrator knows what they're doing.

OTHER PROBLEMS WITH MAIL

If you get complaints from friends that their mail to you is "bouncing" (coming back recipient unknown) or if you experience other problems, contact your own mail administrator. If you are on a small network, you probably know the administrator personally. On a larger network, send mail to postmaster or to postmaster@*your.address* and ask them to look into your problem.

CAUTION

If you go away for a stretch and make no special arrangements, your inbox can literally overflow and you might end up losing mail. Even if you don't max out your inbox you can end up causing big problems for your mail administrator.

Some bounce messages only tell you that a server along the route is still attempting to send the mail. Not every system on the Internet is up and running 24 hours a day.

If you reply to someone's message and your reply comes bouncing back, check the To: header. It's possible that your correspondent's

mail program or system is incorrectly configured and that their address is being garbled. Make sure the address on your message that bounced looks like a correct Internet address, of the form *username@something.something.thing* (or maybe just one dot). If not, resend the message but edit the To: header manually.

WHAT'S NEXT?

Chapter 4 will explain how to use two common mail programs and help you figure out how to use other programs as well. Chapter 5 will introduce you to the phenomenon of online mailing lists and help you find lists based on your interests. The rest of the book will tell about other forms of online discussion and where to find information and programs on the Internet. Naturally, e-mail is still the foundation; thus, many of the specific sites or services on the Net will be identified by a Web address, an e-mail address, or both.

$

CAUTION

Your Mail Program

FAST FORWARD

SET UP YOUR MAIL PROGRAM ➤ *pp 72, 74-75, 87-90*

1. Put your program on the desktop or the Start menu for easy access.
2. Tell your program your e-mail address and full name.
3. Tell your program where to send and pick up your mail.

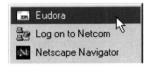

RUN YOUR MAIL PROGRAM ➤ *pp 76-77, 90*

If necessary, connect to your Internet service provider first, and then:

- Click the Start button and choose your mail program, *or*
- Double-click the mail program's icon on your desktop.

Martha Conway	11:40 AM	9/2/
Brendan Houlihan	01:59 PM	9/2/
Gibralto@aol.com	08:50 PM	9/2/
Martha Conway	08:46 AM	9/3/
Beth Dyer	11:00 AM	9/3/
edward justin d'arms	11:59 AM	9/4/
Christian Crumlish	11:13 AM	9/4/
Chris J. Ullsperger	02:55 PM	9/4/
Christian Crumlish	11:48 PM	9/4/

READ MESSAGES IN YOUR INBOX ➤ *pp 77-78, 90-91*

1. Select a message in your inbox.
2. Press ENTER (or double-click the message).

```
>Can you recommend a good e-mail
>have Microsoft Exchange, which c
>Eudora is easier. Which would yc

I rely on Eudora the most, but I
Network-related e-mail.

        --xian
```

REPLY TO A MESSAGE ➤ *pp 77-78, 92*

1. Select a message.
2. Press CTRL-R.
3. Delete as much of the quoted message as possible (retain enough to provide context).
4. Type your reply.
5. Click the Send (or Queue) button.

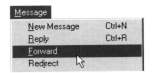

FORWARD A MESSAGE ➤ *pp 78-80, 92*

1. Select a message.
2. Select Message | Forward or click the Forward button.
3. Delete as much of the quoted text as possible, if the entire message is not needed.
4. Type a message explaining why you're forwarding the message.
5. Click the Send (or Queue) button.

DELETE A MESSAGE ➤ *pp 81, 94*

1. Highlight a message (or select several).
2. Press DELETE (or click the Trash button in the Eudora In mailbox window).

REALLY DELETING DELETED MESSAGES ➤ *pp 81, 94*

- In Eudora, select Special | Empty Trash.
- In Exchange, select messages in the Deleted Items folder and press DELETE.

Click Yes if asked to confirm.

SEND A NEW MESSAGE ➤ *pp 81-82, 95-96*

1. Press CTRL-N.
2. Type an address for the recipient (or type a name from your address book).
3. Tab to the Subject line and type a subject.
4. Tab to the message area and type the message.
5. Click the Send button (or the Queue button).

ATTACH A FILE TO A MESSAGE ➤ *pp 86-87, 97-98*

- In Eudora, press CTRL-H, select a file, and click OK.
- In Exchange, click the Insert File button, choose a file, and click OK.

There are a multitude of e-mail programs out there, and there's no way I could do them all justice in this chapter (hey, I'm a busy person too!). Fortunately, aside from idiosyncrasies of command names and window positions, most e-mail programs work more or less the same way. In this chapter I'll show you two of the most common programs, Eudora and Microsoft Exchange. You can get a version of Eudora for free (from the Internet, of course), and a minimal version of MS Exchange comes with Windows 95, with an Internet module available in the Microsoft Plus! Pack.

If you're already set up using a different program, you should still be able to follow most of these instructions, though you may occasionally have to hunt around for the right menu or command.

KEY SETUP INFORMATION

No matter what mail program you use, you'll have to tell it certain things about your e-mail account. If you work in an office, there ought to be someone there who can supply the correct information, but you may be able to figure it out for yourself. Most of what you have to enter is based on your username and Internet address. For example, if you need to supply a POP account, enter your full e-mail address. For your SMTP server (that's the machine that handles your outgoing mail), you can probably enter the part of your address after the @ sign. (If not, your service provider will inform you of this—call your tech support if necessary.) For your return address, again enter your full e-mail address. If you need to supply a dial-up username (so your mail program can log in to your account to get your mail), include only the username portion of your address (up to but not including the @ sign).

You should only have to set up your mail program once (unless you change service providers).

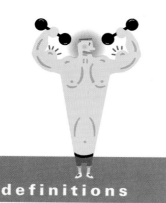

definitions

POP: *Post Office Protocol. Refers to a standard method of storing and retrieving e-mail that Eudora understands.*

SMTP: *Simple Mail Transport Protocol. The most common method of distributing e-mail on the Internet.*

READING MAIL

In most e-mail programs, new mail appears in a window called your inbox. Inboxes generally list just the subject lines of each message. You have to select and open a message to actually read it. Messages are considered new until you've opened (and presumably read) them.

CHECKING FOR NEW MESSAGES

Most e-mail programs automatically check for new mail when you start them up, and then again at regular intervals that you can set (in the Options dialog box for Exchange, in the Switches dialog box for Eudora). However, you can check mail manually any time you want.

In Eudora or Exchange, press CTRL-M to check for new messages.

REPLYING TO MESSAGES

Depending on your outlook (and workload), replying to messages is either the most enjoyable part of e-mail or a tedious burden. Either way, I recommend replying to routine messages as quickly as you can (so you can delete them and forget about them), but only checking your mail a few times a day.

definition

freeware: Software that's free to download and use, as opposed to shareware, which is free to download, but for which you are expected to pay a licensing fee if you continue to use it after a trial period.

netiquette

If you're too busy to respond to e-mail in a timely fashion, consider sending a brief message saying that you did receive the mail and that you'll respond at length when you have the opportunity.

SAVING MESSAGES

Saving has a slightly different connotation with e-mail from the one you're used to. Messages are automatically saved for you until you delete them, but if you want to keep a message around for informational or other purposes, I'd recommend moving it to a folder (or mailbox, depending on the nomenclature of your program). In both Eudora and Exchange you can create storage folders on the fly.

Pegasus Mail is another pretty good free e-mail program that you might want to try. Download it from http://www.cuslm.ca/pegasus/index.htm.

DELETING MESSAGES

As with saving, deleting means something slightly different when speaking of e-mail messages, as opposed to files. Generally, deleting an e-mail message means moving it to a deleted messages area, not unlike the Recycling Bin on the Windows 95 desktop. These messages are then deleted either when you quit the mail program or when you manually delete them from the holding area.

SENDING NEW MAIL

You don't have to reply to existing mail, of course, to send out a new message of your own. Every mail program has a New Message command of some sort.

GETTING AND SETTING UP EUDORA

To get the freeware version of Eudora, point your Web browser at http://www.qualcomm.com/quest/freeware.html and follow the instructions on that page. (Be sure to download the Windows version of Eudora and not the Mac version.) Save the downloaded file (it's a self-extracting compressed file) in a new folder and then double-click it to install Eudora Light. (The commercial version of Eudora is called Eudora Pro.)

If you plan to use your mail program a lot, you may want to put a shortcut to the Eudora program on your desktop or Start menu.

The file is named Weudora, so you might want to change the name of the shortcut to Eudora or something even simpler, such as Mail.

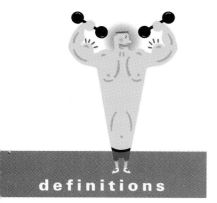

definitions

shortcut: In Windows 95, an icon that points to a program, document, or folder elsewhere on your computer.

winsock: Also Winsock, a Windows driver that enables network software to perform Internet transactions in the Windows operating system.

The first time you run Eudora, you'll have to enter some information about your e-mail account. To do so, select Special | Configuration.

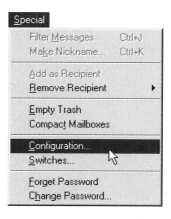

In the Configuration dialog box, enter your full e-mail address, your real name, your SMTP server, and your return address (see Figure 4.1).

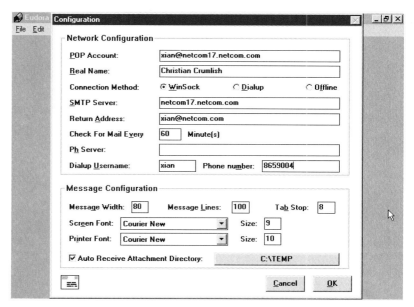

Figure 4.1 Besides entering your username and e-mail address all over this box, you can also select a connection method, tell Eudora how often to check for new mail, and assign a folder for incoming attached files.

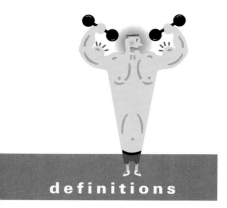

SLIP: Serial Line Internet Protocol. The first popular method of connecting a PC directly to the Internet. There is now also CSLIP (Compresses SLIP), which compresses headers and makes faster use of a modem.

PPP: Point-to-Point Protocol. The most common method for connecting a PC to the Internet. It compresses header information, resulting in faster (than SLIP) communication over a modem.

If you have network access or a PPP or SLIP dial-up account (see Appendix A if you really want to know what all that means), select the WinSock connection method. Otherwise, select Dialup. (If you choose Dialup, you'll have to enter the number you want to dial in the Phone number box at the bottom of the Network Configuration area.)

To assign a folder for incoming attached files, check Auto Receive Attachment Directory and click the button next to it. Choose a folder (Eudora still calls them directories) and then click the Use Directory button.

When everything looks good in the Configuration dialog box, click OK.

Starting Eudora

As with any other program, you run your mail program by double-clicking the program icon (or a shortcut to it), or by selecting it from the Start menu.

When you connect to Eudora, it will immediately check your account for new mail, unless it's set to check for mail every 0 (zero) minutes.

After starting Eudora, you're probably going to read new incoming mail or send new outgoing mail (or maybe do both). I'll explain the procedures for reading mail first, but if you're eager to send a message, feel free to skip ahead.

Reading Mail in Eudora

In Eudora, a new message appears with a bullet in the first column (see Figure 4.2). To read a message in Eudora, select the subject line and press ENTER (or double-click it). The message will open in its own window (see Figure 4.3).

Replying in Eudora

To reply to a message (it doesn't have to be open, just selected), select Message | Reply.

Eudora will start a new message for you and supply the recipient's name in the To: line. It will also quote the original message for you

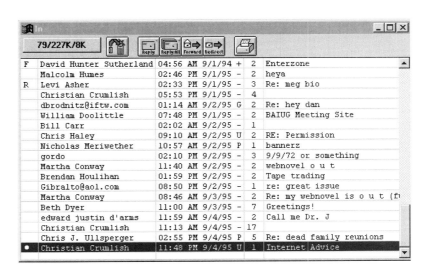

Figure 4.2 There's only one new message in my inbox, and it's automatically selected for me.

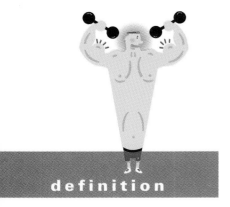

switch: *Switch is just a UNIX-geeky term meaning option, from the image of flipping a switch one way or the other.*

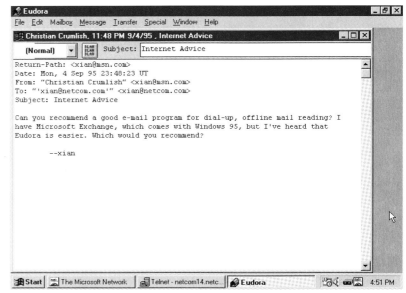

Figure 4.3 An e-mail message in Eudora

unless you've told it not to in the Switches dialog box. Erase any part of the message you don't need to repeat and then type your reply (see Figure 4.4). When you are done, click the Queue (or Send) button.

The difference between Queue and Send is that Queue just adds the message to a list (a queue) of messages and then sends them all at once next time Eudora checks for new mail. Send sends the message immediately. If you prefer the Send approach, select Special | Switches and check Immediate Send in the Sending area of the Switches dialog box (see Figure 4.5).

Forwarding in Eudora

Sometimes you'll want to send a reply not to the original sender, but to a third party instead. To do so, select Message | Forward.

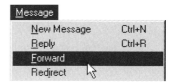

CAUTION

If you're working with Eudora off-line and you check Immediate Send, then every time you complete a message and click the Send button, Eudora will try (and fail) to connect.

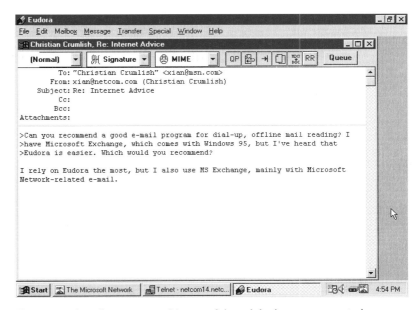

Figure 4.4 A reply message with part of the original message quoted

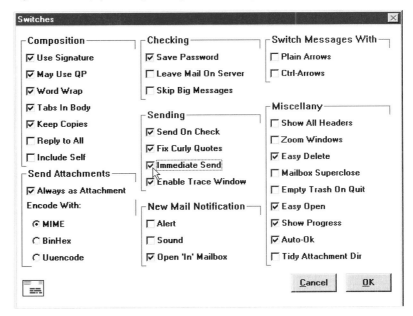

Figure 4.5 Choose Immediate Send in the Switches dialog box to avoid queueing messages. This dialog box controls all of Eudora's optional behavior. Experiment with the other choices to see how they work and how you like them. (Not all the choices shown in this dialog box exist in Eudora Light, but most do.)

Eudora will quote the original message as in a reply but will leave the To: line blank for you to enter the new addressee.

Saving Messages in Eudora

To move a message to a mailbox in Eudora, select Transfer | *the folder name*. At first, there won't be any choices besides the In, Out, and Trash mailboxes. To create a folder, select Transfer | New.

In the dialog box that appears, type a name for the new mailbox.

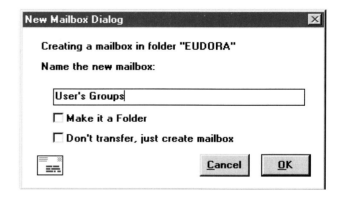

Check the "Make it a Folder" option if you might eventually want subcategories within that folder. Then click OK. You can open a mailbox at any point by choosing it from the Mailbox menu.

A new window will appear, showing the contents of the box you selected.

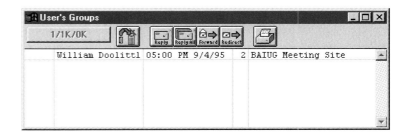

Deleting Messages in Eudora

To delete a message in Eudora select it and click the Trash icon on the top panel of the mailbox window. The message will be moved to the Trash mailbox. (You can also select a number of messages and delete them all at once.)

To empty the trash in Eudora, select Special | Empty Trash.

Sending a New Message in Eudora

To send a message in Eudora, select Message | New Message. Eudora will start a message for you in a new window. Here's a sample message that I composed (the circled numbers on the screen correspond to the numbered steps that follow).

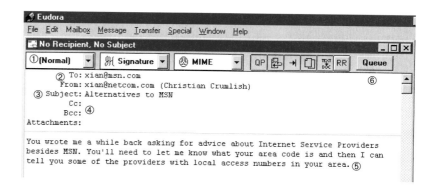

1. To change the priority of the message (from Highest to Lowest) click the first drop-down list box in the top panel of the window, the one that says (Normal).
2. Type an address on the To: line.
3. Press TAB and type a subject in the Subject: line. Remember that this is the first thing your recipient will see.
4. If you want to send a copy of the message to someone else, put the address(es) in the Cc: line. If you want to send a blind copy (meaning that no other recipients will see the address), put the address(es) in the Bcc: line. Otherwise, if you are ready to compose your message, tab repeatedly until the insertion point appears in the message area.
5. Type your message.
6. Click the Queue or the Send button.

Creating Nicknames in Eudora

Eudora allows you to keep track of e-mail addresses by creating nicknames for them. The easiest way to do this is to start with an existing piece of mail, but you can create a nickname from scratch as well, if you have the address handy. Highlight the message and then select Special | Make Nickname.

CAUTION

Not all mail setups recognize the Bcc: header, so it does not provide perfectly reliable anonymity for your "blind courtesy copy" recipients.

SHORTCUT

You can also just press CTRL-N to start a new message.

In the New Nickname dialog box, type a short, memorable name. If you want to put this person on your "short list" of addresses available from the menus, click "Put it on the recipient list." Then click OK.

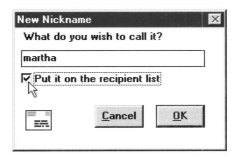

To send (or forward) a message to someone on your recipient list, select Message | New Message To | *nickname* (or Message | Forward To | *nickname*).

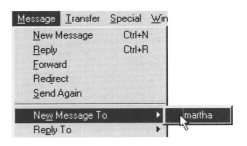

To edit nicknames manually, select Window | Nicknames (yes, Eudora's menu organization makes no sense at all—it's not you!).

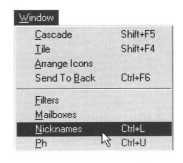

This brings up the Nicknames window (see Figure 4.6). Double-clicking a nickname adds it to the recipient list (and puts a checkmark next to the name). To make a new nickname, click the New button and then type the address in the Address(es): list box. Press CTRL-S to save changes to nicknames and close the window by clicking the Close button in the upper-right corner of your screen (or click the To button to send a message to the selected address).

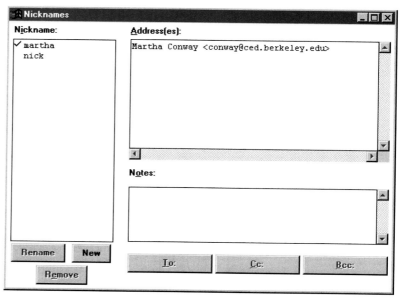

Figure 4.6 Enter, edit, or remove nicknames in the Nicknames dialog box.

Creating a Signature in Eudora

Eudora enables you to set up a signature file to be appended to the end of each message. To create a signature, select Window | Signature.

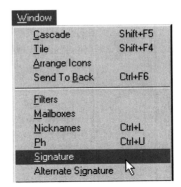

netiquette

It's traditional in Internet e-mail to begin a signature block with two hyphens on a line by themselves. Some mail software looks for those characters as the beginning of the signature.

A small text window will appear. Type whatever you want to appear at the end of each message, press CTRL-S, and then close the window (click the Close button).

```
Signature                                                    _ □ ×
--
christian crumlish
writer, painter, editor, publisher, etc.
```

When sending a message, click the Signature drop-down list box to choose to include the signature or to omit it (Eudora Pro also allows an alternative signature).

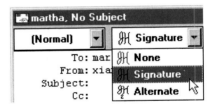

Attaching a File in Eudora

To attach a file to Eudora, select Attach Document.

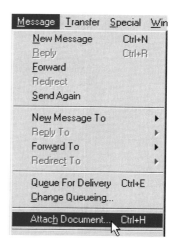

This brings up an Attach Document dialog box much like any old Windows 3.1 Open dialog box (meaning it won't recognize your desktop as the top level). Choose the file you want to attach, browsing through folders as necessary, and then click OK. One nice design feature of Eudora is that it will remember where you looked last, next time you attach a file (see Figure 4.7).

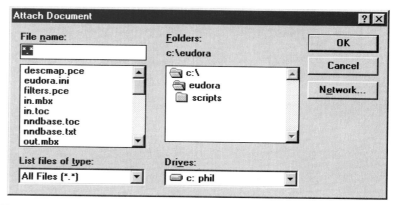

Figure 4.7 Choose a file in the Attach Document dialog box and then click OK.

You can attach more than one document to a message (just repeat the process), but some recipients will see only the first attachment. Consider creating a compressed file with a program such as WinZip, to send all your files in one attachment.

In the third drop-down list box in the top panel of the New Message window, you can choose an encoding method for your attached file. The options are MIME (Multipurpose Internet Mail Extensions, the standard Internet format) or BinHex (the standard Macintosh format, best used when transferring files to or from a Mac—Eudora was first written for the Macintosh, by the way, which shows in some of its design features). The commercial version of Eudora can also do Uuencoding (another common Internet format). You can choose a default format in the Switches dialog box (Special | Switches, Figure 4.5).

Eudora will list the attached file in the Attachments: line of the mail message (see Figure 4.8).

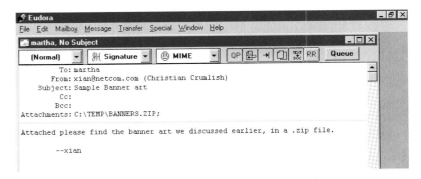

Figure 4.8 Attachments appear listed in the header area of the new message. You can select and delete an attachment if you change your mind.

SETTING UP
MICROSOFT EXCHANGE
(OR MICROSOFT MAIL)

Microsoft Exchange is the mail program that comes with Windows 95. If bought as a separate product (with additional features), it's called Microsoft Mail. I'll just refer to it as Exchange from here on out. Windows 95 automatically comes with an Inbox icon on the desktop that connects to Exchange and opens your inbox. You can put a shortcut to that icon on your Start menu the usual way (though Exchange is already on the Programs submenu of the Start menu).

To set up Exchange for Internet e-mail, select Tools | Services.

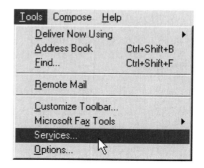

In the Services dialog box, check for an Internet Mail option. If it's already there, click Cancel. If not, click the Add button (see Figure 4.9).

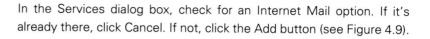

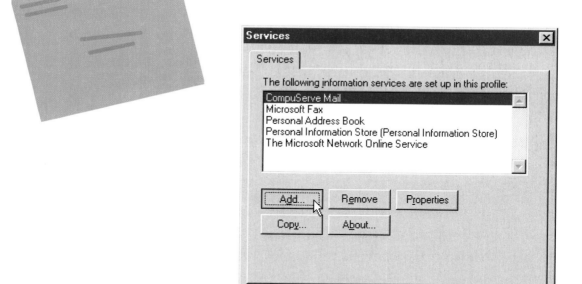

Figure 4.9 Click the Add button in the Services dialog box to add Internet Mail to Exchange.

Choose Internet Mail in the Add Service to Profile dialog box and then click OK.

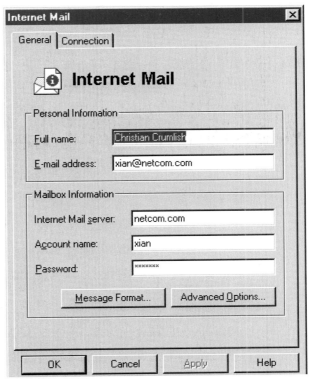

The Internet Mail dialog box will appear. Enter your e-mail address in the Personal Information area and then the latter part of your address (after the @ sign) in the Internet Mail server box, your username (before the @ sign) in the Account name box, and your password in the Password box (see Figure 4.10).

Figure 4.10 Enter your whole e-mail address, and then split it into parts (after and before the @ sign) in the next two boxes.

Click the Connection tab. If you're on a network connected to the Internet, choose "Connect using the network." Otherwise, choose "Connect using the modem" and then select a connection from the drop-down list box (see Figure 4.11).

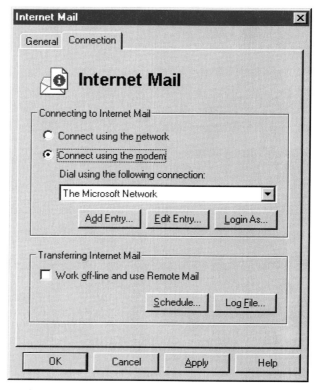

Figure 4.11 Choose the type of connection you have in the Connection tab of the Internet Mail dialog box.

Starting Exchange

You can start Exchange by double-clicking the Inbox icon on your desktop. If you have new mail in Exchange, an icon will appear in the status area at the right end of the Taskbar.

Reading Mail in Exchange

New messages appear in boldface (see Figure 4.12). To read a message, select it and press ENTER (or double-click it). The message will open in its own window (see Figure 4.13).

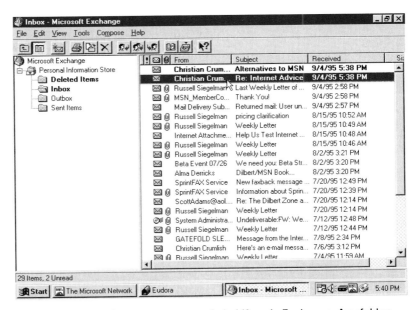

Figure 4.12 Unread messages appear in boldface in Exchange. Any folder with unread messages in it will also appear in boldface in the left pane of the Exchange window.

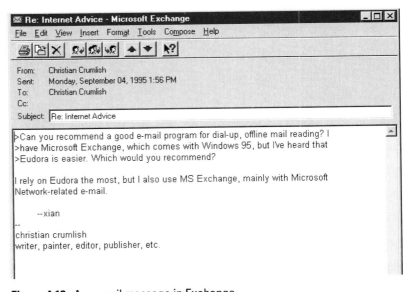

Figure 4.13 An e-mail message in Exchange

Replying in Exchange

To reply to a message, select Compose | Reply to Sender.

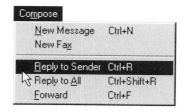

Or click the Reply to Sender button in the message toolbar.

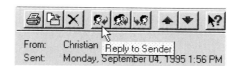

Exchange will start a new message, supplying the recipient's name in the To: box, and quoting the message to which you're replying. Edit the quoted material if necessary, type your reply message, and then click the Send button in the toolbar (see Figure 4.14).

Forwarding in Exchange

To send a reply not to the original sender, but to a third party instead, select Compose | Forward. Exchange will quote the original message as in a reply but will leave the To: line blank for you to enter the addressee. Type a recipient's address or click the To: button and follow the instructions in the "Sending a New Message in Exchange" section, later in this chapter.

Saving Messages in Exchange

To store a message in a folder in Exchange, click the Move Item button in the toolbar.

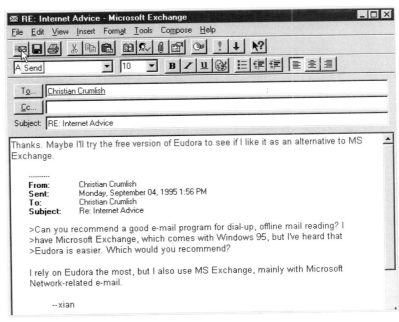

Figure 4.14 Click the Send button to send your reply.

*To hide the left pane, select
View | Folders. (You use the
same command to make it
visible again.)*

The Move dialog box will appear. Choose an existing folder or click the New button.

If you're making a new folder, type a name for it and click OK.

To view the contents of a folder, click it in the left pane of the Exchange window (see Figure 4.15).

Deleting Messages in Exchange

To delete a message in Exchange, click the Delete button on the toolbar. The message will be moved to the Deleted Items folder.

To permanently get rid of messages, just delete them from the Deleted Items folder. Exchange will warn you that these will be permanently deleted.

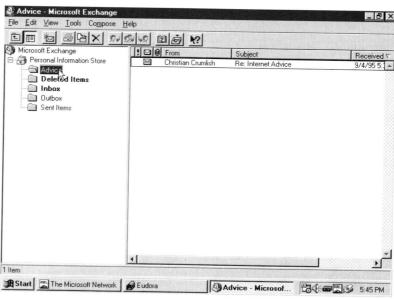

Figure 4.15 Click a folder in the left pane to see its contents.

Sending a New Message in Exchange

To send a new message in Exchange, click the New Message button in the toolbar (or select Compose New Message).

A New Message window will appear. Type an address in the To: box or click the To button to choose an address from (or add one to) your Address Book (see Figure 4.16). The Address Book will appear (see Figure 4.17).

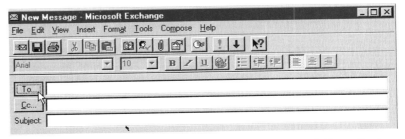

Figure 4.16 Click the To button to add a recipient from your Address Book

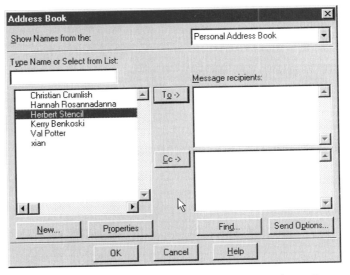

Figure 4.17 The Address Book dialog box lists all your saved e-mail addresses.

Using the Address Book

Choose a name from the list in the left window and click the To button to add it to the recipient list, or click the New button to create a new entry in the Address Book. This brings up the New Entry dialog box (see Figure 4.18).

Select "Internet Mail Address" and then click OK. Type the name and e-mail address of the new recipient and then click the To button to add the address to the To: box of the new message (Figure 4.19).

Tab down to or click in the Subject: box and type a subject line. Then press TAB again or click in the message area and type your message. You can format your message using the buttons on the toolbar (but most of that formatting will not appear if your recipient is not on the same network you're on).

Find Out When Your Message Gets Read

If you're anxious to hear when your message has been received, click the Read Receipt button on the toolbar.

When its recipient opens your message, a message will automatically be sent back to you, to let you know it was received (as long as their mail system cooperates).

If you consider your message to be very important, click the Importance: High (red exclamation point) button on the toolbar.

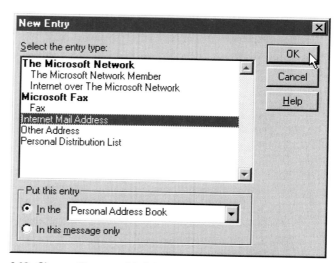

Figure 4.18 Choose "Internet Mail Address" and click OK to add a new address.

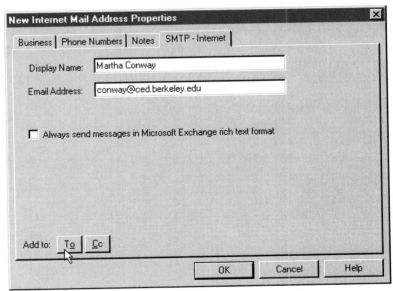

Figure 4.19 Enter the new name and address and then click To.

Attaching a File

To attach a file in Exchange, click the Insert File button on the toolbar.

In the Insert File dialog box that appears, select the file you want to include and then click OK (see Figure 4.20). The file will appear as a shortcut icon in your message.

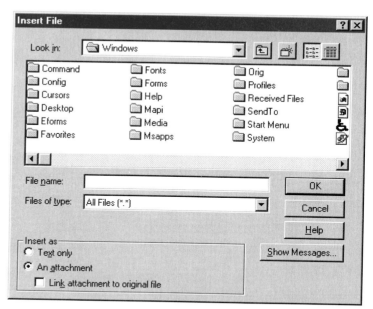

Figure 4.20 Select a file and click OK to insert it into an e-mail message.

SHORTCUT

You can also just press CTRL-M to deliver your messages.

Delivering Your Messages

When you "send" a message in Exchange, it's placed in your Outbox folder. Messages in the folder are not actually sent until you deliver them. To do so, select Tools | Deliver Now (or, if you have more than one type of e-mail connection set up in Exchange, select Tools | Deliver Now Using | Internet Mail).

SETTING UP A VACATION MESSAGE

The ability to send out special vacation messages has not yet spread to most Windows e-mail programs. If your e-mail is handled by a UNIX machine, though, you can go to a useful page on the Web to set up a vacation message and let the Web gateway handle the ugly little UNIX details for you. To do so, point your Web browser at http://charlotte.acns.nwu.edu/mailtools/ (see Figure 4.21).

You'll need to have the same kind of information handy that you used to set up your mail program.

habits & strategies

Open your mail program and look in the configuration or options area for your mail information.

CAUTION

The Mail Tools page requires that you send your password over the Web, which is not secure. Consider changing your password after you avail yourself of this service.

habits & strategies

With Microsoft Exchange's Remote options, you can set up rules for selectively downloading mail from a remote machine. Designed with laptop travel in mind, this approach can also be used to filter mail.

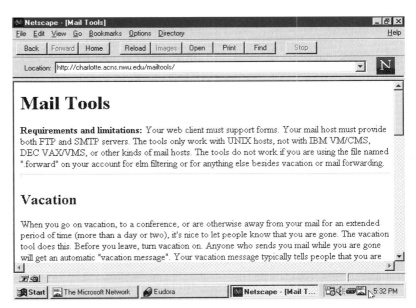

Figure 4.21 The Mail Tools page on the Web. Just scroll through the page and follow the directions. They're pretty straightforward.

AUTOMATICALLY FILTERING AND FORWARDING MAIL

Windows e-mail programs have not really caught up with UNIX standards yet, as far as frills such as filtering and forwarding go. Exchange has no special abilities in these areas, nor does the free version of Eudora. (No matter what mail program you're using, if your mail is handled via a UNIX server, then you can probably both filter and forward your mail, but you'll need a UNIX guru to set it up.)

The commercial version of Eudora enables you to filter your mail automatically. To do so, select Window | Filters.

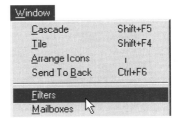

habits & strategies

If you use Word for Windows 7.0 for Windows 95, you can make Word your e-mail editor (as part of the installation process). Then Exchange will automatically invoke Word whenever you create a new message.

Choose a header line for Eudora to base the filtering on, and then describe what should or should not be in the header. Usually, you'll filter mail based on the From: line, the To: line (in the case of mailing list messages), or the Subject: line. You can enter a second criterion if you like by changing the box in the middle from *ignore* to *and* or *or*. If you choose *and*, both criteria will have to be met for the mail to be filtered. If you choose *or*, either one of the criteria will suffice.

Then click the Transfer To box and choose one of your mailboxes from the menu that pops up. All messages that meet the criteria you chose will automatically be sent to that box (see Figure 4.22). Repeat for as many filters as you want to set up. When you're done, press CTRL-S and then close the window (click the Close button).

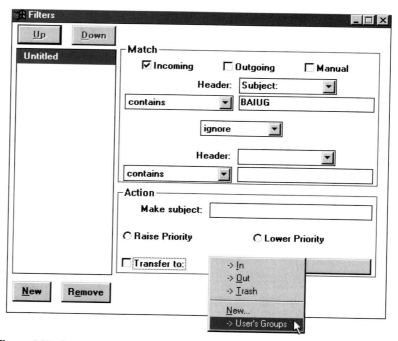

Figure 4.22 Set up an automatic filter in Eudora to sort (at least some of) your mail.

COMPOSING MAIL OUTSIDE OF YOUR MAIL PROGRAM

If you're not completely comfortable in the space provided for composing messages in your e-mail program, you can also write messages in a word processor and then cut and paste them into your mail program (this is different from attaching files).

You have to watch out for the special typesetting characters that modern word processors are forever inserting into your documents, because they will generally appear as garbage characters once the mail has passed over the Internet.

WHERE TO GO FROM HERE

Besides helping you to keep up with all your old college buddies around the globe, e-mail enables you to join mailing lists and participate in online discussion groups. Chapter 5 explains all about lists. Chapter 6 will show you the more public Usenet news groups, which have thousands of additional forums for discussion. Later chapters will introduce the research and file-transfer facilities of the Internet.

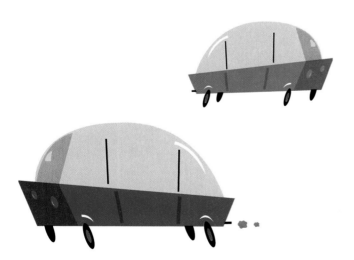

5

MAIL

CA

Mailing Lists

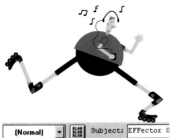

FAST FORWARD

(Normal) ▼ | BLAH BLAH BLAH | Subject: EFFector 0
To: effector@eff.org (effector mailing .
X-Proccessed-By: mail2list

Netscape - [Publicly Accessible Mailing Lists]
File Edit View Go Bookmarks Options Directory

Back | Forward | Home | Reload | Images

Location: http://www.NeoSoft.com/internet/paml/

This is a list of mailing lists available primarily
list is different from a newsgroup because yo
it. To be added to a mailing list, please mail

To subscribe, send the command
    SUBSCRIBE EXOTIC-L your-first-
in the BODY of an email message to
    LISTSERV@PLEARN.EDU.PL

For example: SUBSCRIBE EXOTIC-L Joe

List administrator: katsmith@vt.ed

Last change: Mar 95

A MAILING LIST IS ➤ *pp 107-108*

- An impromptu list of addresses in an e-mail To: header
- An alias (nickname, address-book entry) associated with a list of e-mail addresses
- An e-mail address that corresponds to a list of subscribers

FIND LISTS THAT INTEREST YOU ➤ *p 109*

1. Point your Web browser at the subject index of the Publicly Accessible Mailing List site (http://www.neosoft.com/internet/paml/bysubj.html).
2. Choose a topic that interests you.
3. Note the subscription information for one or all of the lists indexed under that subject.

FIGURE OUT IF THE LIST IS HUMAN- OR ROBOT-ADMINISTERED ➤ *pp 112-113*

The information about the list should include how to subscribe.
If it doesn't, it should at least give the contact address.

- If the contact address starts with listserv@ or majordomo@, and/or if the contact address does not contain the name of the list, then assume that the list is robot-administered.
- If the contact address starts with *listname*-request@, then the list might be administered by a real person, but there's no guarantee.

```
Please add me to the fabulous funny
cars mailing list. Thanks.
```

SUBSCRIBE TO A
HUMAN-ADMINISTERED LIST ➤ *p 112*

Send a message to *listname*-request@*list-address* (not the mailing
list address itself!), asking in plain English to subscribe.

SUBSCRIBE TO A
ROBOT-ADMINISTERED LIST ➤ *pp 112-113*

Send a message to the contact address (often
listserv@*somewhere*, not the mailing list address itself!), typing
subscribe *listname Your Name* on a line by itself, with no
signature or subject. (For some list servers the command is join,
not subscribe.)

```
subscribe FUNCAR-L Herbert Stencil
```

```
Please unsubscribe me from
the fabulous funny cars
mailing list. Thanks.
```

UNSUBSCRIBE FROM A
HUMAN-ADMINISTERED LIST ➤ *p 113*

Send a message to *listname*-request@*list-address* (not the mailing
list address itself!), asking in plain English to unsubscribe.

```
signoff FUNCAR-L Herbert Stencil
```

UNSUBSCRIBE FROM A
ROBOT-ADMINISTERED LIST ➤ *p 113*

Send a message to the contact address (often
listserv@*somewhere*, not the mailing list address itself!), typing
signoff *listname* (or **unsubscribe *listname***) on a line by itself, with
no signature or subject.

BEFORE POSTING TO A LIST ➤ *pp 113-114*

- Lurk for a while to get up to speed with ongoing
  conversations.
- Ask about and read the FAQ (Frequently Asked
  Questions list).

```
1)    WHAT ARE FAQs?
1.1)  What does FAQ stand for?
1.2)  How is FAQ pronounced?
1.3)  What do FAQs contain?
1.4)  What are FAQs used for?
1.5)  Where are FAQs found/kept/
```

```
          To: campervan-etc@lists.Stanford
        From: xian@netcom.com (Christian C
     Subject: Re: Eugene Chadbourne discog
          Cc:
         Bcc:
Attachments:

>Hi -- I was checking out your CVB page,
>maintain a Eugene Chadbourne discography
>http://www.math.duke.edu/~priley/chadbou
>
```

```
set FUNCAR-L nomail
```

REPLY TO POSTED LIST MESSAGES ➤ *pp 114-115*

1. Decide whether the reply should go to the original poster or to the entire list.
2. Use your e-mail program's Reply command.
3. Make sure the address in the To: header is either the individual or the list address (different lists are set up differently), depending on to whom you wish to reply.
4. Trim down as much of the original message as possible.
5. Write your reply and send.

WHEN GOING ON VACATION ➤ *pp 115-116*

Either temporarily unsubscribe to any mailing lists you're subscribed to, or, for robot-administered lists:

1. Send a message to the listserv (or majordomo or listproc) address (*not* the mailing list itself), typing **set *listname* nomail** on a line by itself, and no signature or subject, when you start your vacation.
2. Send a message to the listserv (or majordomo or listproc) address (*not* the mailing list itself), typing **set *listname* mail** on a line by itself, and no signature or subject, when you return from your vacation.

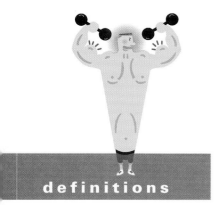

post: A message sent to a public forum of any kind, such as a mailing list or Usenet newsgroup (from the analogy of posting a message to a bulletin board). Also called an article.

thread: An ongoing conversation on a single topic or theme, usually with each message under the same Subject.

One of the Internet's greatest benefits is that it lets you easily find and converse with like-minded people no matter where they're located physically. There are several different types of discussion groups on the Net, but the most basic type is a mailing list.

WHAT'S A MAILING LIST?

A mailing list, often referred to simply as a "list," is made up of e-mail addresses, usually with a single e-mail address set up that forwards all messages sent to it to every address on the list. This facilitates a group conversation in which anyone on the list can participate and which can potentially spawn various threads from a single original post.

Lists do have their downsides as well, especially for a busy person. A high-traffic mailing list will flood your inbox in no time. It's natural to join and quit (subscribe to and unsubscribe from) mailing lists freely, as your interests wax and wane or as the traffic on the list changes.

An Impromptu List

The simplest form of mailing list is simply a list of addressees, separated by commas, on a To: or Cc: line in a message. Anyone who receives such a message and replies to it with their mail program's Reply All command will be posting their reply to the entire original list of addressees. This can become annoying for anyone on the original impromptu list who does not wish to keep receiving follow-up messages, especially because there's no official list and no administrator to appeal to, just a lot of individuals who have the entire list attached to an e-mail message in their mail programs.

A Simple Alias List

The next most simple type of mailing list is a list of e-mail addresses associated with a single alias (or nickname, or address-book entry, depending on your mail program). This is only slightly different

Although similar in many ways to mailing lists, Usenet newsgroups (explained in Chapter 6), do not send posts directly to your mailbox, but instead keep them in a central location you can visit at your own discretion. Mailing lists are often less "noisy" than newsgroups and more often have archives of past articles.

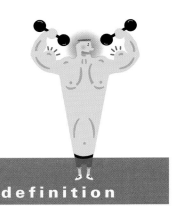

definition

robot: *On the Internet, usually refers to an automated process that may or may not behave like a real person (as opposed to a mobile tin can in a science fiction movie). Also called "bots" or "agents."*

from the first example, because, in this case, the original sender does maintain an official list, but the recipients will all see the expanded list of e-mail addresses on the To: line; so after the first post, the effect is the same.

If you have a group of friends or associates to whom you occasionally wish to broadcast a message, setting up an alias for all their e-mail addresses is a good way to go (just use whatever method you normally use to create an alias, but enter a list of addresses instead of a single one).

A "Real" Mailing List

The most sophisticated type of mailing list is an actual e-mail address associated with a list of addresses. When the mail server of the main address receives incoming mail, it automatically forwards it to every address on the list. Such mailing lists are maintained either by human volunteers or by robotic mailing-list programs (controlled by e-mail commands).

The main thing you need to know before subscribing to a list is whether it is administered by a human or a robot. With human-administered lists, you send plain English messages to the administrator when you want to join the list, quit it, inquire about it, or change your status on the list. With robot-administered lists, you send carefully worded messages that include commands for the program that controls the list.

Digests

Some mailing lists can also be subscribed to in a "digestified" form, meaning that every ten or so messages (or every 20 or 40 kilobytes worth of messages, or all the messages from a single day or a single week) are lumped into a single "digest" and sent out. This can help reduce the number of messages appearing in your inbox for a high-traffic list. Digests often have the feel more of a newsletter—often a very democratic newsletter in which anyone can participate and there is no editor.

Moderated Lists

Some mailing lists have a moderator, a volunteer who screens messages sent to the list and posts only those that are "on-topic" (directly related to the topic of the list) and noninflammatory.

habits & strategies

If your mail program can create a Bcc: line in a message, this is the best place to put an alias to a list of addresses, as none of the recipients will have to see the entire list and the problem of an impromptu list floating around is avoided.

WHAT DO MAILING LISTS OFFER YOU?

There are lists on every imaginable topic—scientific, academic, business-related, music, hobbies, social groupings, television shows, you name it. You might find useful advice and collegiality on a mailing list related to your work or you might find the time to relax and escape your work briefly on a list devoted to your favorite rock and roll band, gardening tips, sport, or what have you.

Supportive lists can link together a community of people who've suffered through something similar and give up-to-date options. For example, real lists help people who've suffered through cancer, diabetes, and miscarriages—and all types of common and rare illnesses—share experiences and trade the names of medicines and therapies that may not be widely known.

How to Find Mailing Lists That Interest You

Because mailing lists are being formed (or dying out) every day, it would be a full-time job to keep up with the entire set of lists. Fortunately, in the Internet community there are many people who voluntarily maintain references to exactly that kind of information. You just have to know where to look.

Probably the definitive source of mailing lists is a document called, naturally enough, Publicly Accessible Mailing Lists, currently in 17 parts.

How to Find Lists on the Web

Point your Web browser at http://www.NeoSoft.com/internet/paml (see Figure 5.1).

Read over the main page and then follow the links for an index by name or by subject (see Figure 5.2).

If you have any trouble connecting to this version of the document, try a site with a slightly less fancy organization (basically just a list of the 17 parts of the document as posted to various newsgroups) at http://www.cis.ohio-state.edu/hypertext/faq/usenet/mail/mailing-lists/top.html or you can try directly accessing the archive site where the posted documents are stored at ftp://rtfm.mit.edu/pub/usenet/news.answers/mail/mailing-lists/ (this site is frequently busy and hard to connect to).

To search for mailing lists, you can also just point your browser directly at one of the PAML indices (at http://www.neosoft.com/internet/paml/byname.html or http://www.neosoft.com/internet/paml/bysubj.html).

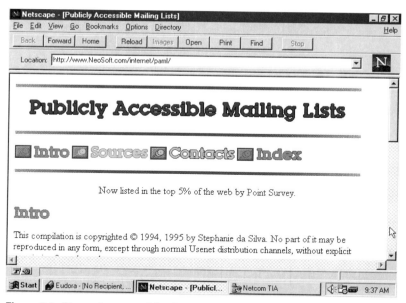

Figure 5.1 The main page of the Publicly Accessible Mailing Lists Web site

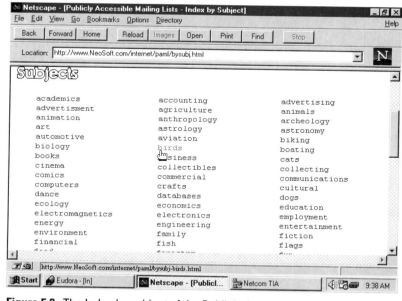

Figure 5.2 The Index by subject of the Publicly Accessible Mailing Lists site

How to Find Lists by E-Mail

If you've tried hunting on the PAML Web page and haven't yet found a mailing list that interests you, you can send for a different index of mailing lists. To do so, send mail to mail-server@rtfm.mit.edu with no subject and no signature. For your message, type

```
send usenet/news.answers/mail/mailing-lists/part01
```

to get the first document in the set. Repeat for part02 through part17.

If you're looking for mailing lists on a specific subject, you can send mail to listserv@bitnic.educom.edu with no subject and no signature. Your message should be just one line:

```
list global / topic
```

but you should replace the word *topic* with the subject you're interested in. Figure 5.3 shows the e-mail I received in return when I sent the command "list global / bird" to that address.

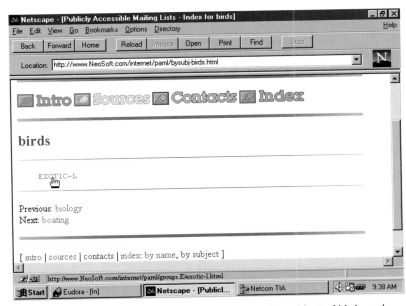

Figure 5.3 Here, I've searched for mailing lists on the subject of birds and come up with one mailing list, EXOTIC-L.

HOW TO SUBSCRIBE

Subscribing to a list means requesting that your e-mail address be added to the list so that all posts to the list are sent to you. The methods vary depending on whether the list is human-administrered or robot-administered.

netiquette

Be very careful not to send a subscription request to the list itself. There is almost always a separate mailing address for such administrative matters.

Human-Administered Lists

For human-administered lists, the administrative address is a variant on the list address, usually the word "-request" appended to the part of the address before the @ sign. So, to subscribe to a (fictional) mailing list called busy@syx.com, you'd send a message to busy-request@syx.com, saying "Please subscribe me to the list." If you get back a reply from a robot, then follow the instructions in the next section.

Robot-Administered Lists

For robot-administered lists (often called list servers or listservs, after the listserv program that maintains the lists), the subscription address is completely different from the mailing list (because it's a central administrative address for a number of lists). The subscription address is often listserv@*such-and-such* or majordomo@*so-and-so*, and your subscription request must be of the form

```
subscribe listname Your Name
```

or, for some listservs

```
join listname Your Name
```

CAUTION

Don't send any of your administrative requests to the mailing list itself. This will annoy all of the subscribers!

Chapter 4 explains how to save a message in a special mailbox or folder in your mail program.

So, to subscribe to the (real) Allergy mailing list, send e-mail to listserv@tamvm1.tamu.edu and in the body of the message put this:

```
subscribe Allergy Your Name
```

If you get back a confusing result or an error message, send a message to the listserv address with just the word "help" in it and you should be sent a complete list of correct commands.

When sending mail to a robot, leave out your signature. It will only confuse the poor thing. (Or you can type the word "end" on a line by itself at the end of your message. Everything after it will be ignored.) Also, leave the subject line blank (it's ignored anyway).

Saving the Subscription Info

When you join a list you're usually sent a welcome message and a set of instructions for unsubscribing and other useful things. Save this message. Create a special folder for it in your mail program and add the similar messages you get from other lists when you join them. Eventually, they'll come in handy.

Unsubscribing

If and when the time comes to quit a list, send your request to the same address you originally sent to when you joined. For human-administered lists, send a message to *listname*-request@*address* asking in plain English to be unsubscribed. For robot-administered lists, send a message to the listserv address, typing **signoff *listname*** (or, if that fails, try **unsubscribe *listname***) and nothing else.

LURKING

Mailing lists (and newsgroups) usually have many more readers than participants. Some of this is human nature. It is considered totally normal (and is actually recommended) that you read a list for a while before you post for the first time. This is called lurking. The purpose of this netiquette is to prevent new people from jumping into the middle of old conversations without understanding the background and ideas that have led up to the current point. Once you get the hang of the topic "threads" and have a feel for who's who, you can contribute more easily without stepping on toes.

definition

RTF: Also RTFAQ, it stands for "read the FAQ" and is a generic answer to frequently asked questions in a mailing list or Usenet newsgroup. (This is roughly the equivalent of responding, when asked the spelling of a word, "look it up in the dictionary.")

FREQUENTLY ASKED QUESTIONS

For every list there are certain questions that get asked most frequently, especially by new contributors (also called newbies). There may be nothing wrong with the questions themselves, but after you've been on a list for a while, it gets tedious to keep seeing (or answering) the same questions. Because of this, a tradition had arisen on the Net for lists and other discussion groups to assemble Frequently Asked Question lists, usually referred to as FAQs (FAQ is pronounced *fack*). FAQs grow often as a collective effort, though usually one person must take responsibility for maintaining the document.

When you join a list, wait or ask for the FAQ to be posted so that you can get answers to the most common questions before piping up with your own. Some FAQs are posted regularly to Usenet and archived at sites accessible from the Web. People on the list will tell you where to look (they'll appreciate you finding the answers to those questions yourself rather than bothering them).

CONTRIBUTING TO A LIST

To contribute to a mailing list, all you have to do is send mail to a list address. If you're responding to a previous post, you can usually just reply in your mailer (but make sure that the To: address is the mailing list and not the individual who posted—this depends on how the list is set up). As with any mail, trim off as much of the quoted material as you can but retain enough to make the context of your reply clear.

netiquette

Keep your posts to mailing lists on topic. It's natural for threads to occasionally "drift" from the main purpose of the list, but take your conversations to private e-mail as soon as they're obviously out of the scope of the list.

habits & strategies

Any time you're replying to a list post, check the To: line of your e-mail message to make sure you're sending the mail where you think you are.

Chapter 4 explains how to set up a vacation message to let your e-mail correspondents know you'll be away for awhile.

Responding Privately

As a general rule, err on the side of replying to individuals instead of to the list as a whole. There's nothing wrong with posting to the list, but some conversations naturally spawn side chats that really have nothing to do with the list. Before you post to a list, ask yourself if you're really just talking to the previous poster. If so, send the mail directly to her or him.

Avoiding Flame Wars

Probably because the communication is not face to face, e-mail makes it easy for people to lose their tempers and send insulting mail to each other. Such messages are called *flames* and when they're sent to a mailing list they can engender a long series of flames and counter-flames, known collectively as a *flame war*. It might be tempting to get in there and mix it up with everyone, especially the first time you see this happening, but it's really a waste of everyone's time. Often the original offense was simply a poorly worded message that a reader construed as an insult. Stay out of flame wars and don't fan the flames.

Some people like flaming so much that they will post deliberately inflammatory messages, called *flamebait*. If you read something that fills you with the urge to immediately reply in terms as scathing as possible, pause for a moment and think about whether that is precisely how the writer hoped you would respond. Don't give them the satisfaction.

If someone misinterprets something you wrote and takes offense, just apologize. No harm will be done and you might make a new friend. Many a flame war has been headed off by a timely apology. Later on, think about what you wrote and be more careful in the future about how you put things.

Going on Vacation

If you'll be away from your e-mail for a while, you may want to temporarily unsubscribe from your mailing lists. Listserv mailing lists have an option that keeps you on the list but halts the sending of mail. To invoke this, send mail to the listserv (or majordomo or listproc) address, typing **set *listname* nomail** on a line by itself. When you return, send a message saying **set *listname* mail** to start the messages coming again. You won't be sent the messages you missed, but if your mailing list has an archive of old articles, you can hunt for them there (if you've got the time).

WHERE TO NOW?

Once you've tried out some mailing lists you'll probably want to explore the largest set of discussion groups on the planet, Usenet. Chapter 6 explains Usenet and Chapter 7 tells you how to work a newsreader to subscribe to, read, and participate in the groups that interest you. Chapter 8 tells you how to have live, real-time conversations. Later chapters cover information and software resources on the Net.

Usenet Newsgroups

FAST FORWARD

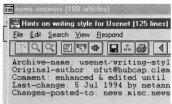

USENET IS ➤ *pp 121-124*
- A set of worldwide special-interest electronic bulletin boards
- A network of networks sharing public messages
- A huge system of discussion groups
- Organized hierarchically
- More or less a synonym for "newsgroups"

USENET IS NOT ➤ *pp 121-124*
- The Internet (though it mostly lives there)
- Part of some online service
- Private
- Accessible only in the U.S.

TO OBTAIN MORE
USENET INFORMATION ➤ *pp 124-125*
1. Check out the Usenet Info Center FAQ.
2. Read the articles in the news.answers newsgroup.
3. Spend some time lurking in newsgroups before posting questions.

CAUTION

You've probably heard the words *Usenet, Netnews,* and/or *newsgroups* by now, but you might not be sure what they really refer to. First, all three are more or less synonyms. Usenet is an international network of networks, distributed largely via the Internet but not exactly equivalent to the Internet. There are people not on the Internet with access to Usenet and vice versa. For the most part though, if you have Internet access, you have access to the Usenet newsgroups.

Usenet stands for User's Network, and it's often spelled in all capital letters, at least on the Net. Netnews is a synonym for Usenet, referring to the news system in general. Articles posted to Usenet discussion groups are often referred to as "news" or Usenet news, although the analogy to newspapers is not a perfect one. The discussion groups likewise are called newsgroups. The contents of newsgroups are contributed by the readers, who post articles and respond to previously posted articles in the group or by e-mail.

Before the Web's soaring popularity, Usenet was the biggest attraction on the Internet. Because of its interactive nature, Usenet still constitutes the public space of the Net, where ideas are hashed out and personal relationships are formed. If there is an Internet culture, it derives largely from the communication in Usenet newsgroups (along with e-mail and live chatting).

A large number of newsgroups are technically not part of the Usenet system. From your point of view, the only real difference will be that non-Usenet newsgroups are not carried as widely or as consistently by some Internet service providers. I'll go into more detail about distinguishing Usenet from non-Usenet groups later in this chapter.

For more background on Usenet check out a highly informative document called the Usenet Info Center FAQ, available on the Web at http://sunsite.unc.edu/usenet-i/info-center-faq.html (see Figure 6.1).

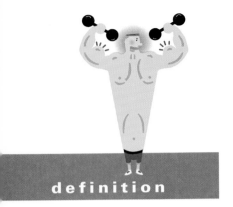

definition

FAQ: *A Frequently Asked Question list, usually created collaboratively by the members of a discussion group (such as a mailing list or newsgroup) and maintained by volunteers.*

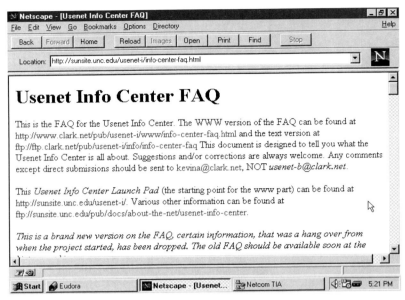

Figure 6.1 The Usenet Info Center FAQ

ACCESSING USENET

One advantage newsgroups have over mailing lists is that the messages (articles) posted to them do not appear in your mailbox, but are instead stored in a central location. All your computer or software has to keep track of is which messages you've already seen. After a while messages "expire" and disappear from the news server. The flip side of this is that most mailing lists maintain archives of past articles, whereas Usenet articles more often disappear for good when they expire.

To continue with the news metaphor, deciding to read a group regularly is called "subscribing" to it, even if all that means is that the name of the group appears in your regular list whenever you run your newsreading program. (That is, you still won't see the articles in the newsgroup unless you explicitly check for them.)

Because news posts propagate outward from the author's news server to the rest of the news servers on the globe, you can't always be sure that you're seeing articles in the same order in which they were written. This can lead to threads that go in circles as old comments are reiterated.

Chapter 7 will explain the nitty-gritty of reading newsgroups, through a variety of methods. You'll see how to read Usenet through an online service such as the Microsoft Network, how to do it with a Web browser such as Netscape, and how to run specific Windows newsreader programs (see Figure 6.2).

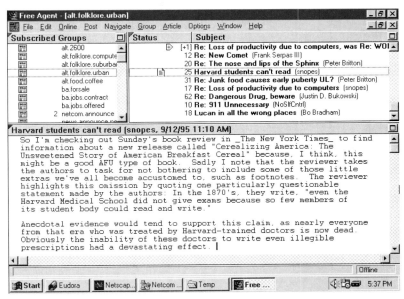

Figure 6.2 Reading a newsgroup in Free Agent for Windows

USENET AND ALTERNATIVE NEWSGROUPS

One expert estimates that, taken together, there are now over 17,000 Usenet and alternative newsgroups (and more are created every day).

Newsgroups are organized hierarchically, into categories and subcategories. Ideally, this is to help you find the newsgroup you want, but it's not always clear where to look. In the official Usenet hierarchies, there are seven main categories (see Table 6.1). Categories are divided into newsgroup names by dots, UNIX-style, so the newsgroup for discussing the Microsoft Windows operating system, for example, is called comp.sys.os.mswindows.

There are assorted other top-level hierarchies that comprise the non-Usenet newsgroups. The most popular is the *alt* hierarchy (alt stands for alternative), where many of the more provocative newsgroups can be found. These non-Usenet newsgroups work about the

CAUTION

Users with female (or female-sounding) names or usernames may experience unwanted solicitations from male adolescent-types just for posting publicly. It's best to develop a thick skin about this kind of thing or affect a gender-neutral username. This problem is worse in the most controversial, sex-related, newsgroups.

See Chapter 10 for more on searching the Net for specific information.

Newsgroup Hierarchy	Meaning
comp	Computers
misc	Miscellaneous (could be anything)
news	News (Usenet news, that is—the Usenet system itself)
rec	Recreation (music, sports, games)
soc	Social (social groups, discussions of society)
sci	Science
talk	Talk (mostly debate)

Table 6.1 The Seven Usenet Hierarchies

same way as the Usenet ones do, but they can be formed much more easily (Usenet requires a formal discussion and voting process), and they are not as well distributed.

PUBLIC DISCUSSION

Usenet is essentially a public space. You should never post anything to a newsgroup that you wouldn't feel comfortable reading in the newspaper. Even e-mail is not as private as it seems, because so many people can look at unencoded e-mail as it happens to pass through their system, but Usenet posts are intended for a public audience and are not suitable for private or sensitive information.

In general, posting publicly can result in e-mail responses. This is fine when you are looking for information or contacts, but it can be a nuisance if you are trying to keep your e-mail under control. If you receive unwanted mail, be polite but firm about not wanting to receive it, and then delete anything else that comes from that same source.

WHERE TO GO FOR INFORMATION

Usenet is not really an information medium, although information abounds on the groups—in other words, it is not a reference library. Because the contents are always shifting and no one is obliged to answer your questions for you, it's difficult to go to newsgroups with a specific question and be sure of finding an answer. Then again, it doesn't hurt to ask.

Remember that the people who contribute to newsgroups do it voluntarily, so if you want to ask a question, try lurking on the group for a while first to see if your question is answered and to get a feel for the preferred mode of discourse there (every group is different!).

There is a joke on Usenet that the best way to get information is to post wrong information and wait for people to correct you. Naturally, people won't appreciate it if you knowingly post incorrect information, but that gives you a sense of at least one dynamic at work on the Net, one-upmanship.

There is a set of newsgroups whose names end in the word "answers" (such as news.answers, misc.answers, alt.answers, and so on) where FAQs and other informational documents are regularly posted. Try looking in these groups when you need an answer. (You can't post questions to these groups—but there are in fact some newsgroups whose names end in the word "questions" where you can.) Figure 6.3 shows the news.answers newsgroup.

USENET "CULTURE"

Some people will barge into a newsgroup, start asking questions, demand answers, and then complain about not being served. The response to this will range from "hey we're not the reference room staff, we live here" to "don't let the door hit your ass on the way out." Newsgroup regulars tend to think of their group as a location, a place where they can expect to see their friends and where people interact in some agreed upon way. Some newsgroups (such as alt.callahans, for example) have elaborate ongoing metaphors that establish an imaginary space (in the case of alt.callahans, a bar that is featured in a series of science fiction stories), and a lot of play-acting. Most groups

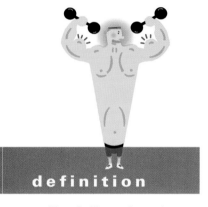

definition

trolling: Deliberately posting incorrect information, for the purpose of eliciting know-it-all responses. Trollers get a big kick out of watching people leap to correct others: "Telly Savalas was not the Captain of the Love Boat!" and so on.

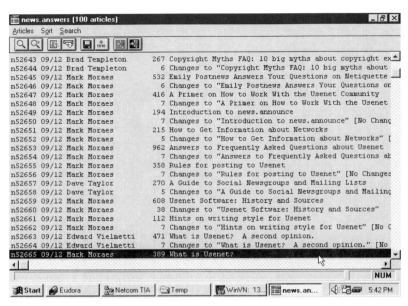

Figure 6.3 Check out news.answers for all kinds of useful information about Usenet itself

don't take the concept that far, but many have cliques, running jokes, and traditions.

Moderated Newsgroups

Some newsgroups, such as the *.answers groups, are moderated, meaning (just as it does with mailing lists) that a volunteer screens all potential posts to the group and passes on only those that are on-topic. Most newsgroups are not moderated (which will become readily apparent to you once you start poking around).

Flames and Flame Wars

As on mailing lists, but even more so, in newsgroups there is always the danger that an insensitive phrasing, a raw nerve, or a deliberate baiting will result in flames, either serious or hilariously exaggerated attacks on another poster, usually egregious. Flames often bring counterflames and sometimes erupt into full-fledged flame wars.

Along with the trollers out there, having fun at the expense of earnest newbies, there are also *flame baiters,* who deliberately post articles that skewer the sacred cow of a particular group. When you are presented with a post that obviously, after a moment's thought, is designed to enrage you, the best reaction is to delete the thing and forget it. The key here is the moment's thought before responding. Don't give flamebaiters what they want.

DIP YOUR FOOT IN THE WATER

OK, I've held you back from the Net long enough. Time to dive in. Chapter 7 has the lowdown on all the how-to's of Usenet and other newsgroups. Chapter 8 will tell you how to converse with people in real time, if that's your thing. After that, we'll get down to business and the rest of the book will tell you how to get information, files, and programs, and where to look.

How to Read Newsgroups

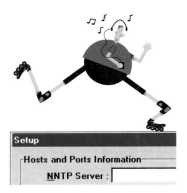

FAST FORWARD

SET UP A NEWSREADER ➤ *p 132*

To set up a newsreader you generally have to supply
- The Internet address of your news server.
- The location of your Newsrc file (if you have one).

READ NEWSGROUPS, IN GENERAL ➤ *pp 132-134*

1. Run a newsreader (or connect from an online service).
2. Subscribe to newsgroups.
3. Select a newsgroup.
4. Choose an article or thread.
5. Read and possibly respond to an article.
6. Move from article to article, and from thread to thread.
7. Post new articles.

READ NEWSGROUPS IN MSN ➤ *pp 135-143*

1. Double-click a newsgroup (BBS) icon.
2. Double-click an article to read it.
3. To respond by e-mail press CTRL-R.
4. To post a follow-up to the newsgroup, select Compose | Reply to BBS.
5. To post a new article press CTRL-N.

READ NEWSGROUPS WITH A WEB BROWSER ➤ *pp 144-148*

1. Enter a newsgroup name in the Location box (in the form news:*newsgroup.name*).
2. Click an article to read it.
- To respond by e-mail, click the name of the author in the From: header of the article.
- To post a follow-up to the newsgroup, click the Post Reply button at the top or bottom of the article window.
- To post a new article to a newsgroup, go to the Newsgroup window and click the Post New Article button at the top or bottom of the article list.

READ NEWSGROUPS
WITH AGENT OR FREE AGENT ➤ *pp 149-150*

1. To select a newsgroup, double-click its name in the Subscribed Groups pane.
2. To read an article, select it in the Newsgroup pane.
- To respond by e-mail, press R.
- To post a follow-up, press F.
- To post a new article, press P.

READ NEWSGROUPS
WITH NEWS XPRESS ➤ *pp 151-152*

1. To select a newsgroup, double-click the newsgroup name in the Newsgroups window.
2. To read an article, double-click the article name in the group window.
- To respond by e-mail, press F8.
- To post a follow-up, press F6.
- To post a new article, press F5.

READ NEWSGROUPS WITH WINVN ➤ *pp 152-153*

1. To select a newsgroup, double-click its name in the main WinVN window.
2. To read an article, double-click its name in the Newsgroup window.
- To respond by e-mail, press CTRL-O.
- To post a follow-up, press CTRL-L in a message window.
- To post a new article, press CTRL-L in any other kind of window.

It's possible to search all newsgroups for key words, but not with a typical newsreader program. See Chapter 10 for how to search the Net in general and Usenet in particular.

There are many different ways to get access to news-groups, but don't let this confuse you—though the way newsreaders look and operate varies, the basic function-ality stays the same. All newsreaders provide a way to display news articles and respond to them in a number of ways. In this chapter I'll first show you, in general, how to operate a newsreader and read Usenet newsgroups, so that no matter what method you use, you'll have some idea of what you're doing. Then I'll demonstrate several different ways to read news—via an online service such as Microsoft Network, through a Web browser such as Netscape, and with several different popular Windows newsreader programs.

THE BASIC NEWSREADING DRILL

More important than learning the specific menu commands and keyboard shortcuts of a particular program, is to first get a feel for what is entailed in reading newsgroups. Then the specific commands and techniques will have a context (plus you can always refer to this chapter if you forget a specific command).

One-Time Setup

Usually the first time you run a newsreader, you have to do some setup. You'll need to know the Internet address of your news server (this can be a name, such as news.net-provider.com, or a number, such as 192.0.2.1). You may also have to set up a file called a Newsrc (the name comes from UNIX) that keeps track of the groups you've sub-scribed to and what articles in them you've seen.

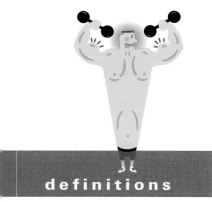

definitions

newsfeed: The "flow" of articles from one news server to the next and from a news server to a newsreader (client program).

thread: An ongoing conversation in a newsgroup, consisting of an article and a series of related follow-ups.

Subscribing to groups is not a one-shot deal. You can add or subtract groups from your subscription list at will.

Subscribing to Groups

Most newsreaders will start you off automatically subscribed to a few informational newsgroups, such as news.announce.newusers, but some will try to subscribe you to the entire list of available groups (depending on your newsfeed, this could easily be over 10,000) and others will start you off unsubscribed to all groups.

Reading the News

Reading the news itself mainly consists of selecting threads and articles to read and ignore (based on their headers), and then reading them. Some groups have a very low signal-to-noise ratio, meaning that there are a lot of useless articles crowded around the interesting ones. With these groups, you do as much news weeding as newsreading.

Navigating the Newsgroup

Not all newsreaders are "threaded," meaning capable of displaying and linking relationships between articles, but most are. With a threaded newsreader you can read an article and then jump directly to an article that replies to it or to an earlier article in the same thread. Outside of threads, navigating a newsgroup consists of moving from article to article.

Marking Articles

Most newsreaders allow you to select the articles you want to read first and then read only those articles. Some let you mark articles as read without actually reading them, as a way of clearing them out. A few newsreaders enable you to grab news headers and then make your article selections off-line, then connect again (briefly) to download only those articles and threads you marked.

Killing Threads

Some newsreaders enable you to "kill" an entire thread, which means marking it so your newsreader will ignore the thread and not show you its headers. This capability can make news weeding a lot easier, especially in very noisy newsgroups.

Responding to Articles

Usenet is an interactive medium, so if an article inspires you to respond, whether to agree or argue, you can do so either by sending mail to the author of the article or by posting a follow-up in the newsgroup. Which you decide to do depends mainly on the context of your reply and whether your follow-up bears directly on the topic of the newsgroup and is of general interest. If your response is of interest only to the author, send a personal e-mail.

Posting a New Article

You can also start your own threads in most newsgroups, without having to respond to an existing article. (See Chapter 6 for guidelines for how and when to jump in.)

Some articles are "cross-posted" to more than one newsgroup and some have a Follow-Up header directing posted replies to a specific newsgroup. Pay attention to where your follow-ups are going so you don't accidentally post where you didn't mean to.

Goodies

There are also a few newsreading extras that not all programs can offer.

Signatures

As with e-mail programs, some newsreaders can append a signature file to the end of your replies and newsgroup posts. It's traditional to keep signatures to four lines or fewer on Usenet.

Off-Line Newsreading

Some newsreaders can function when not connected to the Internet, allowing you to choose threads, read downloaded articles, and compose replies without using any connect time. Then the newsreader can go online briefly to update newsgroups and post your replies.

Now that you know *what* to do, the rest of this chapter will show you *how*. We'll start with an online service.

habits & strategies

Newsreaders that enable off-line newsreading (such as Agent, described later in this chapter) can help prevent a lot of wasted time online for busy people.

READING NEWSGROUPS ON AN ONLINE SERVICE

This section shows you how to read news from the Microsoft Network, but steps for America Online, CompuServe, Prodigy, and the rest will be very similar. (See Appendix B for an introduction to the Microsoft Network.) Most online services nowadays offer access to Usenet (and other) newsgroups, usually referring to them as Internet newsgroups and generally glossing over the distinctions between content unique to the service and contents being piped in from the Net.

If you don't have a MSN (or similar) account, skip ahead to "Reading News in a Web Browser."

Discussion Groups on MSN

As with other online services, the Microsoft Network offers both its own private discussion areas, available only to members of the service, and access to Usenet and Usenet-style discussion groups, using the same tools for both. MSN refers to its own discussion groups as BBSs, alluding to bulletin board systems. (A bulletin board system is essentially a program that runs on a PC and enables multiple users to call in, check e-mail, post and read notes, and maybe also type live conversations or join discussion groups.) A bulletin board with pushpin-posted notes is the central metaphor of the Usenet newsgroups, so MSN's BBS icon is appropriate.

Once you know how to work with a BBS on MSN you know how to read newsgroups, and vice versa.

Reaching the Internet Center

All the newsgroups fed from the Internet can be found in MSN's Internet Center. To find your way there, first click Categories in MSN Central (see Figure 7.1).

In the Categories window, click the Internet Center icon.

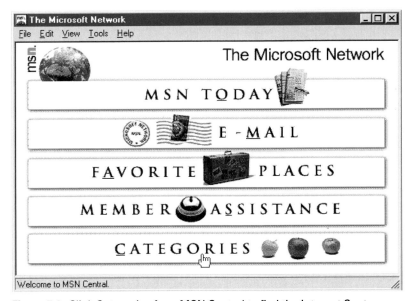

Figure 7.1 Click Categories from MSN Central to find the Internet Center.

Using the Internet Center

The Internet Center window sports a number of icons that feature information about the Internet and Usenet newsgroups. Spend some time clicking the various icons, if you want to brush up (see Figure 7.2).

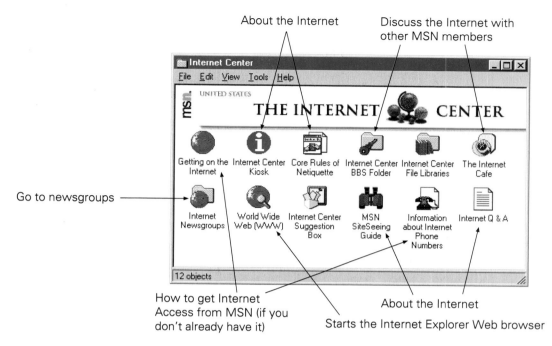

Figure 7.2 Some of the information available in the Internet Center window may prove useful to you, but the Internet Newsgroups folder is where the action is.

Getting to Newsgroups

Double-click the Internet Newsgroups icon. The Internet Newsgroups window appears (see Figure 7.3).

If you double-click the NetNews icon, you might be overwhelmed watching the entire list of available newsgroups filter into a BBS window. Instead, I'd recommend starting from one of the Internet folders:

- Double-click the Usenet Newsgroups icon to read groups in any of the "big seven" Usenet hierarchies (comp., misc., news., rec., sci., soc., and talk.).
- Double-click The Most Popular Newsgroups icon to just dip your feet into a small and manageable number of groups, to begin with.
- Double-click the Other Popular Newsgroups icon to see most of the other (non-Usenet) hierarchies of newsgroups, particularly the alt. hierarchy.

- Double-click Regional & International Newsgroups to see the geographical hierarchies—those that start with an abbreviation representing a nation or place, such as uk. (United Kingdom), ba. (San Francisco Bay Area), and so on.

All newsgroups, alphabetically

Information about Usenet (and other) newsgroups

Internet folders

Figure 7.3 Choose NetNews to select from an enormous list of newsgroups or choose one of the Internet folders to narrow down your choices gradually.

For now, let's start off by double-clicking The Most Popular Newsgroups.

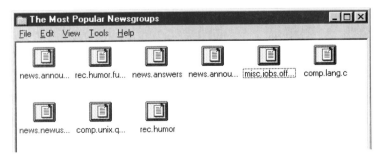

I find it frustrating when the newsgroups' names are not displayed in full, especially when two of them start off with the words news. announce. Worse yet, some of the online services rename newsgroups for the benefit of their users. This leads to their members calling a group by a name most people won't recognize. Double-click news.announce. newusers (the first icon in the window). A BBS window opens (see Figure 7.4).

Subject	Author	Size	Date
Anonymous FTP: Frequently...	Perry Rovers	56.1KB	9/7/95 6:26 AM
DRAFT FAQ: Advertising o...	Joel K. Furr	21.6KB	9/12/95 1:00 AM
Copyright Myths FAQ: 10 bi...	Brad Templeton	12.4KB	9/12/95 1:00 AM
Emily Postnews Answers Yo...	Mark Moraes	24.8KB	9/12/95 1:00 AM
A Primer on How to Work W...	Mark Moraes	21.3KB	9/12/95 1:00 AM
Introduction to news.announce	Mark Moraes	8.49KB	9/12/95 1:00 AM
DRAFT FAQ: Guidelines on...	David.W.Wrigh...	6.72KB	9/12/95 1:00 AM
How to Get Information abo...	Mark Moraes	7.20KB	9/12/95 1:00 AM
Answers to Frequently Ask...	Mark Moraes	43.1KB	9/12/95 1:00 AM
Rules for posting to Usenet	Mark Moraes	18.9KB	9/12/95 1:00 AM
A Guide to Social Newsgrou...	Dave Taylor	12.9KB	9/12/95 1:01 AM
Usenet Software: History a...	Mark Moraes	32.9KB	9/12/95 1:01 AM
Hints on writing style for Us...	Mark Moraes	5.11KB	9/12/95 1:01 AM
What is Usenet? A second ...	Edward Vielmetti	22.8KB	9/12/95 1:01 AM
What is Usenet?	Mark Moraes	17.4KB	9/12/95 1:01 AM

15 conversations, 15 with unread messages

Figure 7.4 Because this is a purely informational newsgroup, you can't post to it (that's why it says "Read Only" in the title bar) and there are no conversations, only single articles.

Adding a Group to Favorite Places

The closest equivalent to subscribing to a newsgroup on MSN is to add a newsgroup to your favorite places. To do so, select File | Add to Favorite Places from the newsgroup window.

To go to favorite places, click Favorite Places in the MSN Central window. (Remember, you can go "up" folder levels in MSN just as with any Windows 95 folders, by pressing the BACKSPACE key.)

Reading the News

To read an article, just double-click its line in the newsgroup window. The message will appear in its own window (see Figure 7.5).

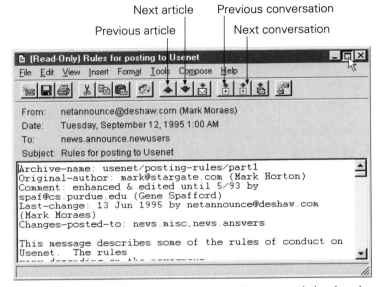

Figure 7.5 Here is an article window. You might have to maximize the window to see the full 80-column line width that's standard on the Internet.

Navigating the Newsgroup

The easiest way to move to the previous or next article in a thread (MSN calls them conversations) is by using the toolbar in a message window. The toolbar also makes it easy to jump to the next or previous thread. These same commands (along with Next Unread Article and Next Unread Conversation) appear on the View menu. There are also keyboard shortcuts (see Table 7.1).

Expanding Conversations

When you enter a newsgroup, all the conversations are collapsed, meaning you only see the first article in the conversation. An article that starts a conversation (and any article with a follow-up attached) is marked with a plus sign in a square. Click the square to expand the next article in the conversation.

To see all the articles in a group, select View | Expand All Conversations. To hide all the extra articles, select View | Collapse All Conversations.

Marking Articles and Killing Threads

Double-clicking an article in a newsgroup window opens the article in a message window and marks it as read (it goes from boldface to plain text). You can also mark articles or entire conversations as read from the Tools menu.

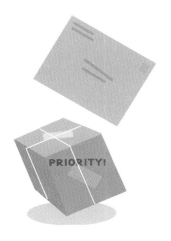

Responding to Articles

You can reply to a message either by using the Compose menu or (if replying to the BBS) by clicking a button on the toolbar.

To Go to the	Press
Previous article	SHIFT-F5
Next article	F5
Next unread article	F6
Previous conversation	SHIFT-F7
Next conversation	F7
Next unread conversation	F8

Table 7.1 MSN Newsreading (BBS) Shortcuts

Responding by E-Mail

To reply to an article by e-mail, select Compose | Reply by E-mail (see Figure 7.6).

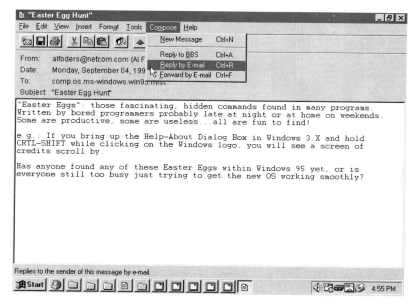

Figure 7.6 Replying to a message by e-mail (instead of posting to the group)

A (Microsoft Exchange) message window will appear with the recipient's name already in the To: field, and the original article quoted. Type your reply and then click the Send button.

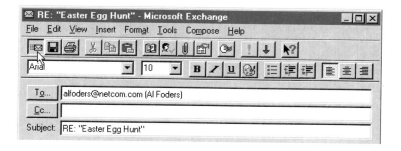

Posting a Follow-Up

To post a follow-up to the newsgroup, click the Reply to BBS button in the message toolbar or select Compose | Reply to BBS.

Posting a New Article

To post a new article, without reference to any previous messages, you can click the New Message button in any message window. Select Compose | New Message in the newsgroup window. Type your message and then click the Send button (see Figure 7.7).

SHORTCUT

You can also press CTRL-N *to post a new message.*

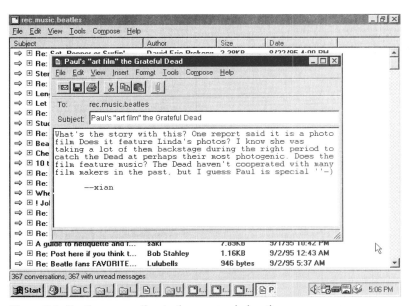

Figure 7.7 Posting a question to the rec.music.beatles newsgroup

MSN Newsreading Miscellany

Don't make the mistake when posting to a newsgroup of thinking that your audience is all Microsoft Network customers. Remember that your MSN window onto the newsgroup is just one of many.

MSN does not yet enable the use of signature files, nor does it allow you to set up automatic kill files to avoid certain conversations. Nor is there currently any facility for off-line newsreading.

Now that you've had a chance to see how to read news in a somewhat sheltered environment, try it using either your familiar Web browser or, best of all, a program especially designed for newsreading.

READING NEWS IN A WEB BROWSER

Web browsers are not quite full-fledged newsreader programs, but they can perform most of the critical functions. Netscape has an especially well-designed news interface.

One-Time Setup

Microsoft Internet Explorer tries to access newsgroups via MSN and this is not customizable.

As with any newsreader, you have to tell Netscape the name or address of the news server from which it should get its feed. To do so (after writing down the correct information), select Options | Preferences and click the Mail and News tab. Enter the address of your news server in the News (NNTP) Server box in the News area at the bottom of the dialog box, as shown here:

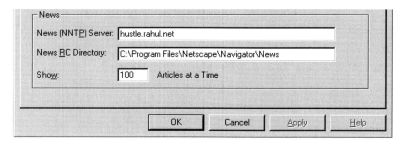

Subscribing to Groups

To start reading the news in Netscape, select Directory | Go to Newsgroups (or type **newsrc:** in the Location box). Netscape looks for a Newsrc file. If it can't find one, it offers to make one for you.

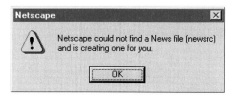

Click OK. Netscape takes you to a page called Subscribed Newsgroups and lists the groups you're subscribed to. If Netscape created your Newsrc file, then you'll at first be subscribed to news. announce.newusers, news.newusers.questions, and news.answers (see Figure 7.8).

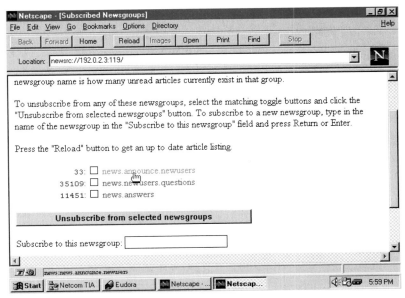

Figure 7.8 This is the bottom of the Subscribed Newsgroups page. You can click a newsgroup name to go to that newsgroup, and subscribe and unsubscribe to newsgroups.

To add a newsgroup to your subscription list, type its name in the "Subscribe to this newsgroup" box on this page. To unsubscribe from any subscribed groups, check the box next to the name of the group(s) and then click the "Unsubscribe from selected newsgroups" button.

Reading the News

To start reading a newsgroup, click its name as indicated in Figure 7.8, or type the name of the group into the Location box (starting with news:). If you jump directly to a group this way, you can add it to your subscription list by clicking the Subscribe button that will appear at the top of the window.

Newsgroup: rec.music.beatles

To read an article, simply click its title in the list of articles (see Figure 7.9).

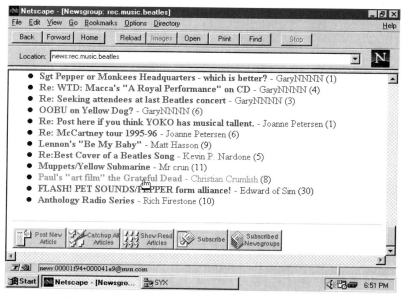

Figure 7.9 Clicking an article (the one I posted from MSN)

Navigating the Newsgroup

To get around a newsgroup, you can either use the Back button whenever you want to return to the article list, or you can click the navigation buttons that appear with articles.

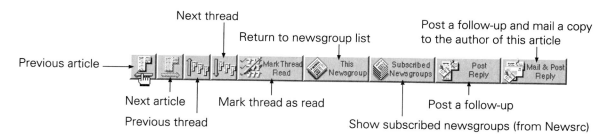

Responding to Articles

You use these same buttons to respond to articles (except for e-mail replies).

Responding by E-Mail

To reply by e-mail, click the name of the author in the From: header of the article. This will bring up Netscape's Send Mail / Post News window with the author's name already in place in the Mail To: box. Otherwise, the procedure is the same as for posting a reply to the group.

Posting a Follow-Up

To post a follow-up article, click the Post Reply button at the top or bottom of the article window.

This brings up a Send Mail / Post News window. If you want to quote from the article, click the Quote Document button at the bottom of the window. You might also want to resize the window so the lines will wrap okay.

Type your reply and trim as much of the quoted article as possible. If you include a Web address in your article, it will appear as an active hyperlink to other people reading news with Netscape. Then click the Send button (see Figure 7.10).

Send Mail / Post News

From: Christian Crumlish <xian@netcom.com>
Mail To:
Post Newsgroup: rec.music.beatles
Subject: Re: Paul's "art film" the Grateful Dead
Attachment: Attach...

```
Sorry to follow up my own post. I also wanted to add that Paul was a
class act not to hype his film in these recent weeks.

xian@msn.com (Christian Crumlish) wrote:
>What's the story with this? One report said it is a photo film Does
                                           oops. forgot a period.

>it feature Linda's photos? I know she was taking a lot of them
>backstage during the right period to catch the Dead at perhaps their
>most photogenic. Does the film feature music? The Dead haven't
>cooperated with many film makers in the past, but I guess Paul is
>special ''-)
>
>        --xian

http://pobox.com/~xian
```

Send   Quote Document   Cancel

Figure 7.10 Posting an article to a newsgroup

To approximate off-line

newsreading with Netscape,

click an article you want to read,

click the Back button, and then

repeat for each article (without

stopping to read them). Netscape

will store those articles in its

"cache." You can now disconnect

from the Internet and read the

selected articles at your leisure.

As with e-mail, Usenet messages carry
headers that enable newsreaders to
sort them and relate them to other
messages. Not all newsreaders,
however, take advantage of all the
available information, so each
newsreader offers a different subset
of possible features.

Posting a New Article

To post a new article to a newsgroup, go to the newsgroup window and click the Post New Article button at the top or bottom of the article list.

Netscape Newsreading Miscellany

Netscape does support signature files. (Select Options | Preferences, click the Mail and News tab, and enter the name of the sig file in the Signature File box in the Mail area.)

Most Web browsers cannot make use of kill files (lists of threads to ignore), nor can you read news off-line with a Web browser.

NEWSREADERS FOR WINDOWS

There are numerous newsreaders for Windows, and there will probably be more and more all the time. Each of them works differently and has different specific commands, but they're all trying to do the same job. I'll explain three of the most popular newsreaders in the rest of this chapter.

Where to Find Newsreaders

For each of the newsreaders covered in this section, I'll tell you exactly where on the Web you can go to download the latest version. If for any reason you have trouble connecting, this might mean that the location has changed. In that case, either perform a Web search for the name of the newsreader you're looking for (searching is explained in Chapter 10), or go to a central page of Windows Internet applications (often listed under WinSock), such as the Consummate Winsock Applications (http://cwsapps.texas.net/).

How to Read Each Table

The rest of this section will cover three Windows newsreaders—Agent (and Free Agent, the freeware version of Agent), News XPress, and WinVN. For each of these, I'll show you a typical screen depicting the program in action and a table of information. The table will tell you

- How to get the newsreader
- How to do the one-time setup
- How to subscribe to groups
- How to select a newsgroup
- How to read articles
- How to navigate a newsgroup
- How to mark articles and kill threads
- How to respond by e-mail
- How to post a follow-up
- How to post a new article
- Pluses and minuses of this newsreader

Agent/Free Agent

Agent

Agent seems to be the most full-featured new Windows news-reader, and they give away the Free Agent version of the program for, uh, free.

netiquette

A longstanding practice of software developers on the Internet is to make available a free less-fully functional version of a program (such as Eudora Light versus Commercial) and also to beta-test new software by making it available for free to download. If you opt for the more expensive version of a program, you usually get more features and technical support. This is similar to the shareware arrangement, by which you can try out a program for free but are morally obliged to pay for it if you continue to use it. You can minimize your chance of encountering bugs by paying for commercially released software.

Figure 7.11 shows Free Agent displaying an article in the alt.folk-lore.urban newsgroup.

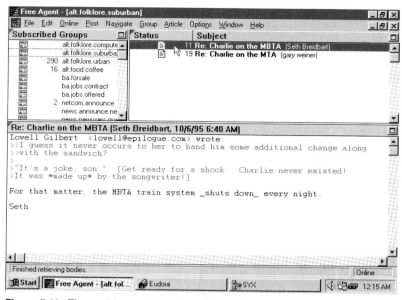

Figure 7.11 The positions of Free Agent's window panes are customizable.

Agent pluses: Multiple signature files, thread selection and killing, off-line newsreading, single-window design. Agent minuses: Almost too many options (confusing), single-window design takes some getting used to.

The following table gives the essentials for Agent and Free Agent:

Where to get it	http://www.webpress.net/forte/agent/
Set it up	By using Options | Preferences (it prompts you for setup information the first time you run it).
Subscribe to a group	By using Group | Show All Groups. To select a group, press CTRL-S. (it also unsubscribes a subscribed group.)
Select a newsgroup	By double-clicking its name in the Subscribed Groups pane.
Read an article	Select it in the newsgroup pane (go online—press CTRL-O—if nothing happens).
Navigate a newsgroup	Then use the navigate menu (keyboard shortcuts listed on menu).
Mark articles and kill threads	Article menu (keyboard shortcuts listed on menu).
Respond by e-mail	Press R.
Post a follow-up	Press F.
Post a new article	Press P.

News Xpress

News Xpress is a popular freeware Windows newsreader. Figure 7.12 shows News Xpress displaying an article in the comp.os.ms-windows.win95.misc newsgroup.

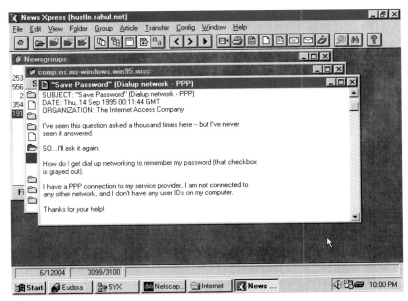

Figure 7.12 News Xpress's window layout is much like any other Windows program, with a main window and any number of document windows inside it.

News Xpress pluses: Allows signatures, very easy thread kill and autoselect, off-line newsreading, free. News Xpress minuses: Slightly buggy (but pretty stable for freeware!).

The following table provides the essentials for News Xpress:

Where to get it	ftp://ftp.hk.super.net/pub/windows/Winsock-Utilities/
Set it up	Use Config | Setup (it prompts you for setup information the first time you run it).
Subscribe to groups	Use CTRL-G to show all groups, ALT-S to subscribe, and ALT-U to unsubscribe.
Select a newsgroup	File | Connect. Then double-click the newsgroup name in the Newsgroups window.
Read an article	Double-click the article name in the group window.
Navigate a newsgroup	Use Previous article, Next article, and Next unread article buttons in the toolbar.

Mark articles and kill threads	Press CTRL-R to mark as read, press CTRL-U to mark as unread. Ignore threads with Group	Kill/Autoselect.
Respond by e-mail	Press F8.
Post a follow-up	Press F6.
Post a new article	Press F5.

Winvn

WinVN

WinVN is the longest-running popular Windows newsreader, based on an old UNIX newsreader called VN (for visual news). Figure 7.13 shows WinVN displaying an article in the rec.music.beatles newsgroup.

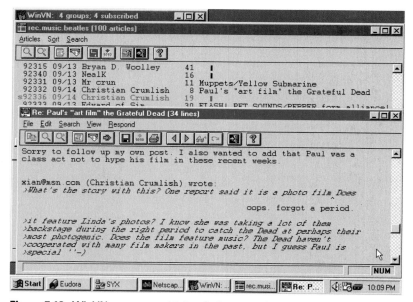

Figure 7.13 WinVN spawns multiple windows, each with its own Taskbar button. the position of each window can be adjusted and saved.

WinVN pluses: Allows signatures, free.
WinVN minuses: Can't kill threads,
can't work off-line, can't select articles
in advance.

The following table provides the essentials for WinVN.

Where to get it	ftp://ftp.ksc.nasa.gov/pub/win3/winvn
Set it up	Config | Communications and Config | Personal Info.
Subscribe to groups	Config | Group List, check Show Unsubscribed Groups, OK. Then Group | Subscribe Selected Groups (Group | Unsubscribe Selected Groups).
Select a newsgroup	Double-click its name in the main WinVN window.
Read an article	Double-click the article in the newsgroup window.
Navigate a newsgroup	Press CTRL-N for next article. Press CTRL-P for previous article. Press F2 (or SPACEBAR at the end of an article) for next unseen (unread) article. Press F3 for next article with the same subject.
Mark articles	CTRL-click to mark an article as read. No way to mark articles for reading in advance.
Respond by e-mail	Press CTRL-O.
Post a follow-up	Press CTRL-L in a message window.
Post a new article	Press CTRL-L in any window aside from a message window.

LIVE TALK

If leaving messages for other people is not immediate enough for you, Chapter 8 will show you how to carry on conversations live (mostly by typing, that is).

INFORMATION, PLEASE

The rest of the book (after Chapter 8) shows you how to search for and where to find information, files, and free programs.

Real-Time Conversation with IRC

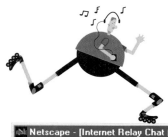

FAST FORWARD

WHAT IS IRC? ➤ *pp 158-160*

IRC (Internet Relay Chat) is a system that permits real-time typed conversations among Internet users, in discussion areas called channels.

A TYPICAL IRC SESSION ➤ *pp 160-162*

1. Run an IRC client.
2. Connect to a server.
3. List channels.
4. Join a channel.
5. Type conversation.
6. Quit.

CHAT WITH mIRC ➤ *pp 162-164*

1. Download mIRC from ftp://cs-ftp.bu.edu/irc/clients/pc/windows (the mirc folder).
2. Unzip and install the program.
3. Run mIRC.
4. Proceed as with any IRC chat.

CHAT WITH WSIRC ➤ *pp 164-165*

1. Download WSIRC from ftp://cs-ftp.bu.edu/irc/clients/pc/windows (the wsirc folder).
2. Unzip and install the program.
3. Run WSIRC.
4. Enter a server to connect to.
5. Proceed as with any IRC chat.

CHAT AND DISCUSS
WEB PAGES WITH NS CHAT ➤ *pp 166-169*

1. Download Netscape Chat from http://home.netscape.com/ comprod/chat_install.html. (Don't type that last period—it's part of the sentence.)
2. Double-click the downloaded file to uncompress it.
3. Run the Setup program.
4. Start Netscape Navigator.
5. Use the toolbar buttons to connect to a server and join conversations.
6. Visit Web pages with the URL bar at the bottom of the window.

CHAT AND VISIT
WEB PAGES WITH GLOBAL CHAT ➤ *pp 169-171*

1. Download Global Chat from http://www.prospero.com/ globalchat/windows/.
2. Save the Globlcht icon to its own folder.
3. Run a Web browser.
4. Run Global Chat.
5. Use the toolbar buttons (down the left side of the window) to connect to a server and list and join conversations.
6. Select a URL and click the Websurf button to send your browser to that address.

Besides the post-office and bulletin-board methods of communicating, the Internet also has facilities for "real-time" interactive conversation. First there was a program called *talk* that enabled two users to carry on sentence-by-sentence conversations. Next came *chat,* which enabled multiple users to communicate this way. The current live-talk infrastructure on the Internet is called IRC, which stands for Internet Relay Chat. As with many other Internet facilities, IRC is a client-server system in which individuals run client programs to connect to centralized servers (and thence to other users).

I can't wholeheartedly recommend IRC to anyone who's really busy, because it can be a slow form of communication (with lots of stray conversations passing through), and because it can suck you in so that hours go by without your noticing. On the other hand, when my Internet Dictionary was being translated into Portuguese in Brazil, the translator needed to ask me some questions and we found e-mail to be slow going (we were sending many messages back and forth each day). We agreed on a convenient time to get on IRC and had our conversation that way. So used cleverly, IRC can facilitate your busy schedule.

IRC EXPLAINED

The basic unit of conversation on IRC is called a channel. At any given moment there are thousands of channels active (and anyone can start a new one at any time). Interested users join the channel and communicate among themselves. You can type messages to everyone on the channel or send private messages to individuals.

For more background information on IRC see the IRC FAQ on the Web at http://www.kei.com/irc.html or a central reference to IRC Related Documents (http://ftp.acsu.buffalo.edu/irc/WWW/ircdocs.html).

CAUTION

There are a lot of adolescent types on IRC and you'll see many channels with bizarre names and lurid descriptions. Remember that the purpose of a system like IRC is to allow people to talk about what they want without getting in anyone else's way, so just ignore any channels with topics that bother you.

IRC Lingo

Once you get on IRC you'll hear a lot of unfamiliar jargon. Here's a quick briefing on some essential IRC jargon:

Expression	Means
nick	A nickname, your name on IRC (not necessarily your username.)
channel	An IRC discussion area.
whisper	Send a private message.
channel operator	The person who created the channel (also channel op, chanop).
kick	To throw someone off an IRC channel (must have channel operator privileges to do this).
bot	A program designed to behave like a person on IRC, a robot.
netsplit	A temporary breakdown in the server network which results in the apparent disappearance of some participants in a conversation. Netsplits usually fix themselves.
motd	Message of the day.
lag	A delay between sending a message and seeing it show up in the channel.
MorF?	Are you male or female? (Asking is considered gauche by some.)

The Undernet

When you run an IRC client, you have to connect to a server, but the server you choose does not completely limit who you can communicate with. Large numbers of servers are allied in one of two networks. When you connect to a server, you can join any channel created on any of the servers networked to your server. The traditional IRC network is called EFnet. There is a newer network called the Undernet that is smaller in scale and more cooperative in its administration. Both are worth visiting. The Undernet touts itself as an alternative to the traditional network.

For more information on the Undernet, see http://www.undernet.org:8080/~cs93jtl/Undernet.html or the Undernet IRC FAQ (http://www.undernet.org:8080/~cs93jtl/underfaq/).

Finding Servers

Some client programs will present you with a list of servers or at least a suggested or default server. Others will leave it up to you to supply a server name. Here is a short list of servers to try if none are suggested by your program:

```
irc.bu.edu
irc.colorado.edu
irc.uiuc.edu
```

For the Undernet, try these:

```
austin.tx.us.undernet.org
manhattan.ks.us.undernet.org
milwaukee.wi.us.undernet.org
pittsburgh.pa.us.undernet.org
sanjose.ca.us.undernet.org
rochester.mi.us.undernet.org
tampa.fl.us.undernet.org
washington.dc.us.undernet.org
```

If you're outside the U.S. or want to see a more complete list of servers, check the IRC Servers List at http://www.funet.fi/pub/unix/irc/docs/server.lst.

IRC SESSIONS IN GENERAL

No matter what IRC client program you run, your chat session will work something like this. First you'll run your client. Next, you'll connect to a server (this may happen automatically). Then you'll want to see a list of available channels. The most basic way to do this is to type **/list** at the prompt. Channel names all start with the # character and the list of channels also tells you how many people are currently on the channel (including bots, if any) and what the channel's topic is.

Next you'll join a conversation. You do this by typing **/join channel name**. Say hello and start "talking" (that is, typing). To send a private message to someone else, type **/msg their-nick your message**.

habits & strategies

If you're prompted for a port number and none has been suggested, try 6667.

habits & strategies

Some channels you might want to visit are #newbie (where you can ask IRC-related questions) and #initgame (where you can practice your IRC skills playing a guessing game).

Slash Commands

Traditionally, all IRC commands start with a slash (/). Some of the new graphical IRC programs offer shortcut menus and buttons as well but most decent IRC programs recognize all or most of the traditional slash commands. Table 8.1 shows a list of essential slash commands that will work with any standard IRC client program.

Command	What It Does
/away *message*	Tells people you're not able to read or respond to the conversation right now.
/help *command*	Gives information about a command.
/ignore *nick*	Screens out unwanted communication from *nick*.
/join *#channel*	Connects you to *#channel* or starts it if it does not currently exist.
/leave *#channel*	Disconnects you from *#channel*.
/list	Lists all current channels.
/list -min *x* -max *y*	Lists all current channels with at least *x* participants and no more than *y*.
/msg *nick*	Sends a private message to *nick*.
/nick *newnick*	Changes your nick to *newnick*.
/query *nick*	Starts a private conversation with *nick*.
/quit	Disconnects from the server.
/who	Lists users on the current channel.
/whois *nick*	Gives known information about nick.

Table 8.1 IRC Survival Guide

IRC Chat

Here's a typical IRC session, using mIRC:

1. Connect to a server. (Decide if you want to connect to the EFnet network or the Undernet. Beyond that, choose a server geographically near to you.)
2. List channels. It's often easier to digest the list that shows up if you limit the channels to just those with between, say, 3 and 4 users.

3. Join a conversation. (Type **/join #channel** or double-click the channel name.)

4. Chat away. Say hello, read the conversation, and jump in when you have something to say.

STANDARD WINDOWS IRC CLIENTS

The two most popular Windows IRC clients are mIRC and WSIRC. (The WS in WSIRC stands for WinSock. I asked the author of mIRC, Khaled Mardam-Bey, what the m in mIRC stands for, and he claims not to remember.) Both are free. (WSIRC also has a shareware version with additional features.) In this section I'll tell you where to get them, how to set them up, and any special features unique to these programs.

mIRC

mIRC is an excellent Windows IRC client. While it has once or twice frozen up on me (what Windows programs don't?), overall it's pretty solid. It has an elegant layout, with each separate task or listing appearing in its own window, all behaving the way normal windows should. There are lots of excellent toolbar shortcuts, and you can right-click on many items and choose from pop-up menus appropriate to the context. Try it.

Where to Get It

To get a copy of mIRC, point your Web browser at ftp://cs-ftp.bu.edu/irc/clients/pc/windows and choose the mirc folder (see Figure 8.1).

Download the most recent copy of mIRC from the folder.

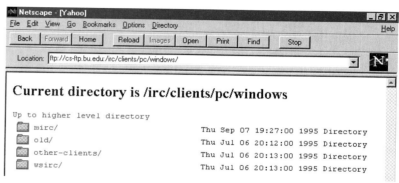

Figure 8.1 The FTP directory containing both mIRC and WSIRC

Installation and Setup

To install mIRC, simply unzip the downloaded file into its own folder. (If you don't have a program that can uncompress ZIP files, download a shareware copy of WinZip from http://www.winzip.com/winzip/download.html, and then try again.)

The first time you run the program, press CTRL-E to choose a server and enter your nick. mIRC comes with some server addresses preloaded.

Running mIRC

To run mIRC, double-click the mIRC32 icon.

Then click the Connect icon (the lightning bolt) or select File | Connect. Once you list channels (using the /list command), the list will appear in a new window. You can join a channel the usual way (with the /join command) or by double-clicking a channel name.

Then type in the pane at the bottom of the window. The channel conversation will scroll through the large pane just above (see Figure 8.2).

To leave a channel, just close the window it's in or use the /leave command. Exit the program the normal way.

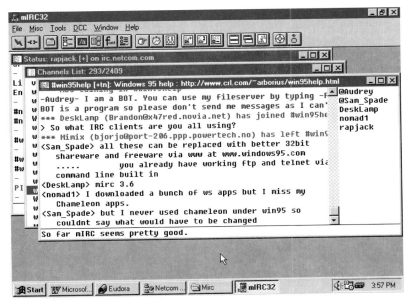

Figure 8.2 Chatting with mIRC on the #win95help channel

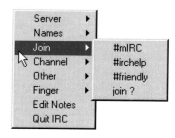

Shortcuts and Unusual Stuff

mIRC has a toolbar featuring essential commands and a number of options available on a pop-up shortcut menu by right-clicking.

WSIRC

WSIRC is a fairly easy-to-use IRC client that automates some typical IRC procedures and provides mouse-click shortcuts while recognizing traditional slash commands. It has some minor bugs, such as the fact that the child windows sometimes resize themselves even if you've maximized them.

The latest version of WSIRC (version 2.0) incorporates support for video-phone style communication. To take advantage of it, you'll need a microphone and sound card.

Where to Get It

To get a copy of WSIRC for evaluation, point your Web browser at ftp://cs-ftp.bu.edu/irc/clients/pc/windows and choose the wsirc folder (see Figure 8.1). Download the latest version of the WSIRC package.

Installation and Setup

Uncompress the ZIP file. (If you don't have a program that can uncompress ZIP files, download a shareware copy of WinZip from http://www.winzip.com/winzip/download.html and try again.) Then run the WSIRC installation program.

Wsirc

WSIRC will install itself in the folder you choose, along with a second freeware version of WSIRC (you can continue to use the freeware version even if you decide not to pay for the shareware version), an uninstall program, help information, and auxiliary files. WSIRC will also set itself up in a submenu of the Start | Programs menu.

To set up WSIRC, just run it for the first time. WSIRC will prompt you to enter server information. Then its help information will appear on the screen. Read as much as you need and then close the window. Enter a server name (or accept the suggested one), and enter a nick for yourself. Then click OK.

Wsirc

Then start your IRC session or exit and return when you're ready to chat.

Running WSIRC

When you start WSIRC it first runs a program called WS-IDENT (ignore this—it's just some setup procedure the program needs to run). Then the WSIRC window appears on the screen with a Server Messages child window inside. When you connect to your server, the message of the day will appear in this window. Each channel will appear in its own window. You might want to maximize the window you're working in but don't forget there are others hidden behind.

Once you list channels (using the /list command or the menu or toolbar shortcuts), the list will appear in the pane along the right side of the window. Click in the pane to widen it so you can read the channel descriptions. You can join a channel the usual way (with the /join command) or by double-clicking a channel name.

Then type in the pane at the bottom of the window. The channel conversation will scroll through the large pane just above (see Figure 8.3).

When you're done with IRC and quit the program, you'll see that the WS-IDENT subprogram is still running. Switch to it and quit it as well.

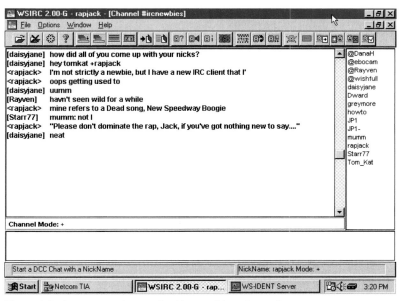

Figure 8.3 A conversation on the #ircnewbies channel

There are also some Web pages with their own sort of Web chat systems that do not take advantage of the IRC networks. This is technically a different kind of chatting.

WEB-ORIENTED CHAT PROGRAMS

A new type of chat program that has only recently begun appearing uses the IRC protocols and servers but interacts with Web pages as well. Unfortunately, the first two programs of this type do not recognize all the IRC slash commands. Perhaps this is just as well for new users, but for people used to IRC, it means relearning procedures for familiar commands.

NETSCAPE CHAT

Netscape has just announced a program called Chat that you can download from the Netscape site. It functions as an add-in program with Netscape Navigator (meaning that the Web browser must be running for the chat program to work).

Besides most of the usual IRC functionality (excluding slash commands!), Netscape Chat also allows users to send Web addresses to each other and to lock their Web browsers together so that a group of people can all visit and comment on the same Web page.

Where to Get It

To get NS Chat, point your Web browser at http://home.netscape. com/comprod/chat.html and read the associated material or go directly to the Netscape Chat Download page (http://home.netscape.com/comprod/chat_install.html).

Download the 32-bit version of NS Chat (see Figure 8.4).

Installation and Setup

To install NS Chat, double-click the downloaded file (it will extract several files from itself) and then double-click the Setup icon. The NS Chat Setup program will start. Click Continue. Choose a folder. The Setup program will install NS Chat.

The first time you run NS Chat, you'll have to enter server information.

Running NS Chat

nschat

You must have Netscape Navigator running to use NS Chat. Once you do, double-click the nschat icon.

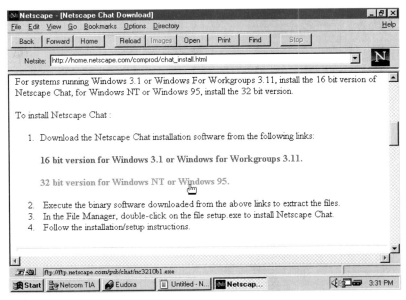

Figure 8.4 Downloading NS Chat

Click the Connect icon on the toolbar (the light bulb) and enter a server as well as information about yourself (just the first time—after that you can just accept the information that's there). Then click OK (see Figure 8.5).

To connect to a channel, click the Group Conversation icon (pictures of voice balloons). To see a list of available channels, click the List button. To connect to a channel, double-click its name (or choose it from the Channel drop-down list box if you've been there before).

The users in the conversation will appear in a pane down the left side of the screen. To whisper to just one user, click their name before typing. To see information about a user, double-click their name (see Figure 8.6).

Touring the Web

If there are other NS Chat users in your channel, they can send Web addresses that your browser will connect to. You can do the same by typing an address in the URL pane at the bottom of the window and then clicking the Send button.

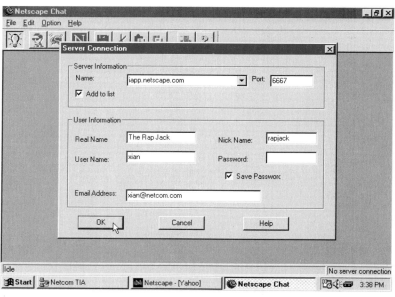

Figure 8.5 Server and personal information for Netscape Chat

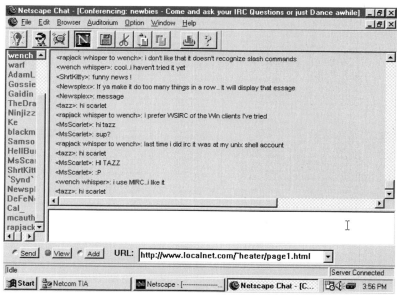

Figure 8.6 A Conversation in NS Chat on the #newbies channel

GLOBAL CHAT

Another entry into the Web/chat market is Global Chat. Global Chat requires that a Web program such as Netscape be running, and enables clickable links on Web pages that launch the program and connect you to a channel. The drawbacks are that it does not recognize most slash commands, and that it displays ads (!) for Web pages while you're chatting.

Where to Get It

To read about and download Global Chat, connect to http://www.prospero.com/globalchat/ (see Figure 8.7)

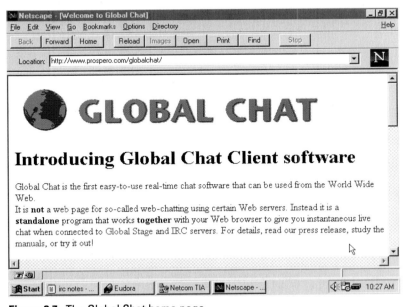

Figure 8.7 The Global Chat home page

You can also go directly to the download directory at ftp://he.net/pub/prospero/globalchat/windows/ and download the latest version of the file. Double-click the file when you've downloaded it (it will extract its contents itself) and move the Globlcht icon to its own folder.

Running Global Chat

To run Global Chat, double-click its icon. Or, if you click on a Global Chat link on a Web page, your browser will ask you what kind of program to use to "view" the link. Tell it to use Global Chat (point to the folder you put it in and click the program icon). From then on, your browser will launch Global Chat whenever you click on such a link.

Click the Sign In button on the left side of the screen to connect to a server. To join a channel, click the Join Channel button. Then chat by typing in the lower pane.

To send a message to just one person, click their name in the pane to the right, choose One Person, and then type your message (see Figure 8.8).

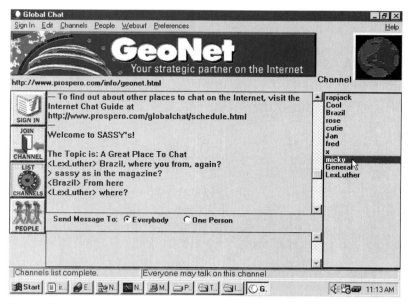

Figure 8.8 Clicking a person's nick prior to sending a message to just that person

Touring the Web

To visit a Web page mentioned in the discussion pane, select it and then click the Websurf button. Click the globe button at the top right to go to the Global Chat home page.

REAL-TIME COMMUNICATION IN OTHER MEDIA

For people with microphones and even video cameras plugged into their computers, there are all kinds of new variations on the IRC model for multimedia communication, including Internet Phone and CU-SeeMe. Because this is a book for busy people, we don't have time to explore those other forms of live chatting, but be aware that they are out there and available. For more information on Internet Phone (IPhone), see The Internet Phone User Directory at http://www.pulver.com/iphone/. For more information on CU-SeeMe, visit the CU-SeeMe Welcome Page at http://cu-seeme.cornell.edu/.

MINING THE INTERNET

The rest of this book will deal not with communicating with other people but with finding information on the Net, connecting to archive sites and other resources, and downloading files and programs.

CHAPTER 9

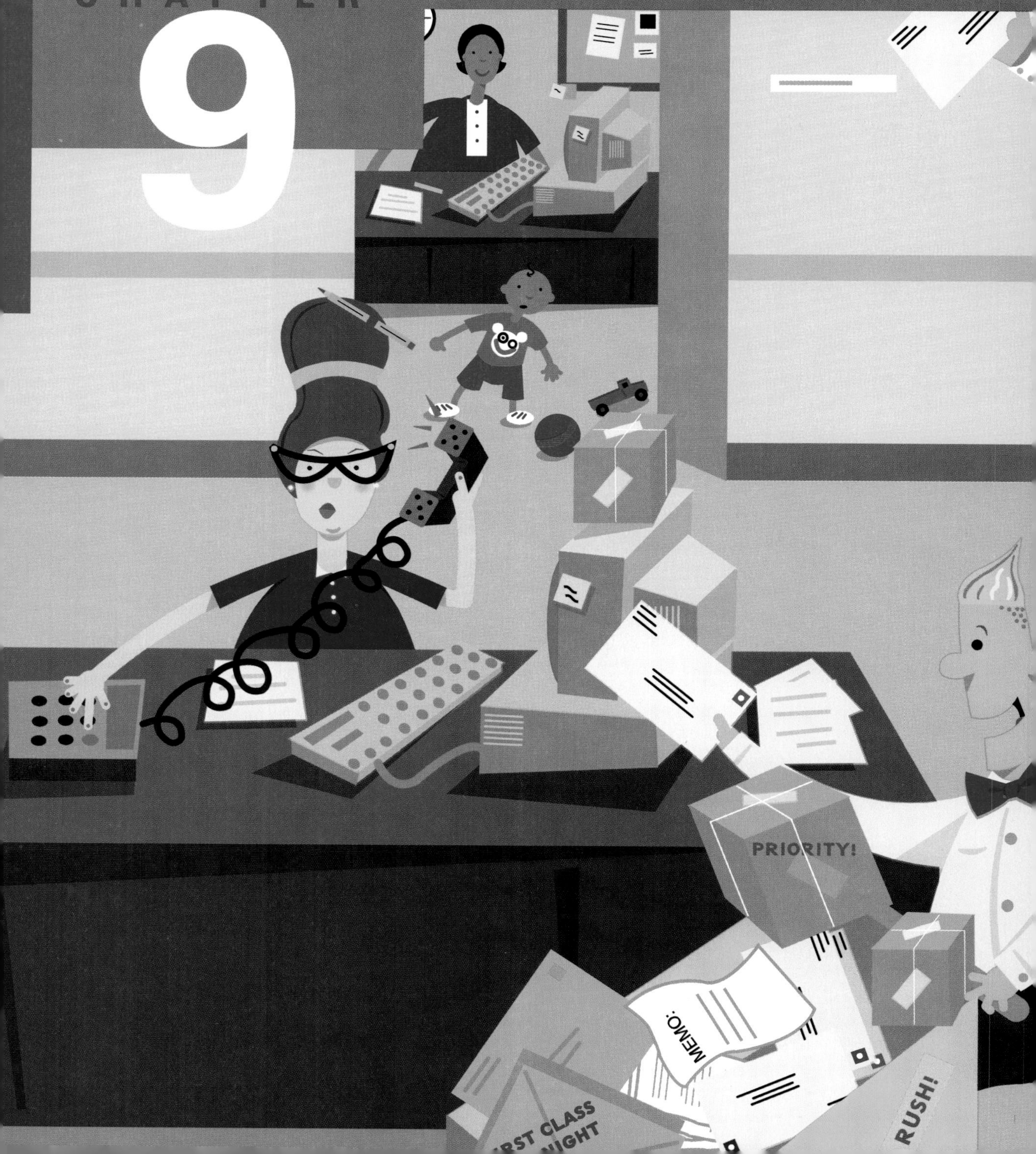

FTP, Telnet, and Gopher: Action at a Distance

FAST FORWARD

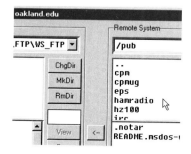

MAKE AN FTP CONNECTION
WITH A WEB BROWSER ➤ *pp 177-179*

1. Enter an FTP URL (in the form ftp://*ftp.site.address/ optional/directory/path*).
2. Click folder links to go to subdirectories.
3. Click document links to download files.

IF A SITE IS BUSY ➤ *p 177*

Try again later, ideally outside of normal working hours.

TRANSFER FILES WITH WS_FTP ➤ *pp 179-183*

1. Choose a site to connect to.
2. Browse to the desired directory.
3. Point WS_FTP at an appropriate folder on your local computer.
4. Double-click the file to be transferred and wait for it to download.
5. Close the connection.

CONNECT TO A TELNET SITE ➤ *pp 183-186*

1. Run the Telnet program that comes with Windows.
2. Select Connect | Remote System.
3. Enter a site name and port number, if necessary, and click OK.
4. Log in, if required.

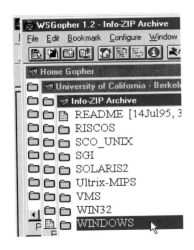

GOPHER WITH A WEB BROWSER ➤ *pp 188-189*

1. Enter a Gopher URL (in the form gopher://
   gopher.site.address).
2. Click folder links to connect to subordinate Gopher menus.
3. Click search icons to search for keywords.
4. Click document links to display or download files.

GOPHER BROWSING
WITH WSGOPHER ➤ *pp 187-192*

- Click folder items to open Gopher menus.
- Click search items (magnifying glass) to search
  for keywords.
- Click document items to display or download files.
- Click the Fetch Bookmark button to choose from a list
  of preset Gopher menus.
- Select Bookmark | Add Bookmark to add the current
  site to a Bookmark list.

175

As an international network of networks, the Internet features numerous archive sites, repositories of software, data, and informative materials. Before the World Wide Web came along and made it so easy to navigate the Net, there were already ways to get to various storage locations and transfer files from them. These older methods still exist and Web browsers have absorbed many of the capabilities of these earlier, specialized programs.

In this chapter, I'll explain FTP (File Transfer Protocol), Telnet, and Gopher, and I'll show you both how to connect with FTP, Telnet, and Gopher sites from within a Web browser, and how to make those connections with programs designed especially for them.

GETTING FILES WITH FTP

I mentioned in Chapters 3 and 4 that you can attach files to e-mail, but except for the occasional, reasonably small file, this is not the most efficient way to transfer files over the Internet. Instead, a protocol was developed for sending and receiving files between computers connected to the Net—the File Transfer Protocol (FTP). FTP is another of the many client-server protocols: individual users run FTP client programs and connect to remote archive sites managed by FTP servers.

Anonymous FTP

There are two ways to use FTP. The first, and less widespread approach, is to log in to an FTP site with a private username and password, and then send or download files to or from the site. The more common use of FTP is called anonymous FTP. An anonymous FTP site is one that permits anyone to log in as "anonymous" without having a special account and password. Anonymous FTP sites are public archive sites. It is more common to download files from public sites than to upload files to them, though both are possible, depending on the rules of the specific site.

Public sites usually can accept only a limited number of connections at a time, so you will sometimes fail to connect when a site is

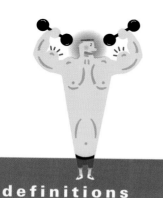

CAUTION

All FTP sites have an upper limit on the number of connections they can handle at once. Whenever possible, try to do your FTP transactions during off hours.

habits & strategies

To make an FTP connection to a nonpublic site, enter the address in the form "ftp://username@site.name." You'll be presented with a dialog box for entering your password. Once you connect, you can download files from the remote site.

busy. Sometimes a "busy" server will display a list of mirror sites. See if any are near you geographically (to minimize your impact on the Net) and try one.

FTP with a Web Browser

Half the time you use FTP from within a Web browser, you'll do it just by clicking on a link that happens to connect to an FTP site. But you can enter FTP addresses directly in the location box, if you write them in the form of a URL. An FTP URL starts with "ftp://" and then has the Internet address of the FTP site. This can be followed by a directory path as well.

Type the URL in the location box and press ENTER. If you try to connect to an FTP site during the workday, you may be refused access. All sites have an upper limit on the number of connections they can handle at once. Whenever possible, try to do your FTP transactions during off hours.

When your browser connects to the FTP site, a special type of page will be displayed, showing a directory listing of the site (and directory) that you're connected to (see Figure 9.1).

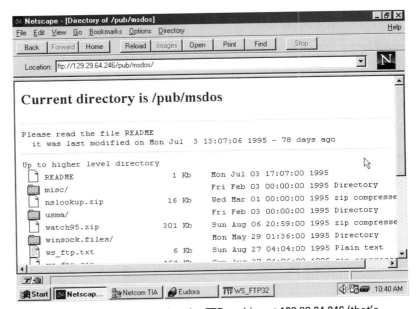

Figure 9.1 I've just connected to the FTP archive at 129.29.64.246 (that's its numerical address—usually you'll be entering a text address) in the /pub/msdos directory, from which the FTP client program WS_FTP32 can be downloaded.

As you might imagine, folder icons represent directories (folders) on the remote machine and document icons represent files. The FTP listing should tell you the type of each file, along with its size, and so on. Click on a directory name to open the directory. Click on a filename to display or download a file.

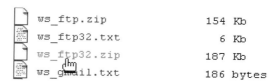

ws_ftp.zip	154 Kb
ws_ftp32.txt	6 Kb
ws_ftp32.zip	187 Kb
ws_gmail.txt	186 bytes

Your Web browser will simply display text files—in fact any kind of file that it recognizes—but will offer to download compressed and executable files.

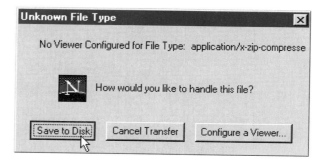

Choose where you want to save the file (and make sure you don't save it as an HTML file).

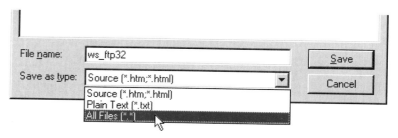

Your browser will keep you apprised of its progress in downloading the file.

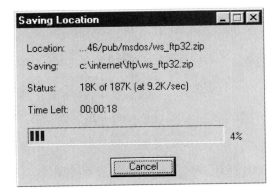

Windows comes with an FTP client called Ftp, but it's a command-line driven program (really a DOS program) and it requires that you know all the UNIXy FTP commands. You're better off using a nice graphical FTP program.

FTP with an FTP Client Program

One thing you cannot do with a Web browser is *upload* a file to an archive site. To do that, you need a full-fledged FTP client. There are a few other advantages to programs designed specifically to do FTP transactions: They usually come with a preloaded list of worthy sites, and they enable you to log into a non-public FTP site (as long as you have a valid password) and send files to the site as well as get files from the site.

WS_FTP

The best FTP client for Windows is called WS_FTP. For Windows 95, you'll want the 32-bit version of the program. You can download it with your Web browser from ftp://129.29.64.246/pub/msdos/, as shown in the previous section. Get the file called ws_ftp32.zip. Save it in or move it to its own folder and then unzip it.

Connecting to Sites with WS_FTP

To run WS_FTP, double-click the Ws_ftp32 icon. The program will start and automatically bring up its Session Profile dialog box. (Don't let the name confuse you—it's for choosing a site to connect to.) It's traditional when logging into a public FTP site as anonymous to offer your full e-mail address as your password. Type your address in the Password box and then check Save Password. If you create a new profile at any time or make any changes to one, check Auto Save Config as well (see Figure 9.2).

habits & strategies

When you run WS_FTP it brings up the Session Profile dialog box automatically. To make a second connection after the first session is completed (and thereafter), click the Connect button in the bottom left.

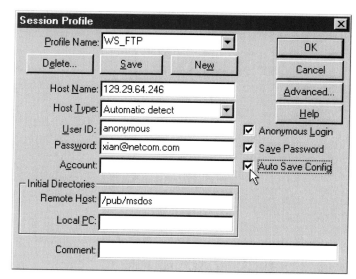

Figure 9.2 Check the WS_FTP site every now and then to make sure you have the most current version of the program.

To connect to a site on the list that comes with WS_FTP, click the Profile Name box and choose the site from the list that drops down (see Figure 9.3). Enter your password (e-mail address) and, if you want, type a path in the Local PC box to indicate a default local folder.

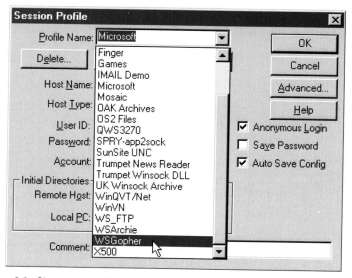

Figure 9.3 Choosing the WSGopher site to download a Gopher client

When you're ready to connect, click OK and WS_FTP will attempt to make the connection.

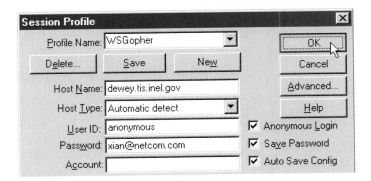

Downloading Files with WS_FTP

Once WS_FTP makes the connection, you are ready to go. The dialog box you will use is split into two main sections (see Figure 9.4). The left side represents your computer, the right side represents the FTP site. On either side, the top drop-down list box shows the current path. The window below the path is split into two panes—the top pane displays directories, and the bottom pane displays files.

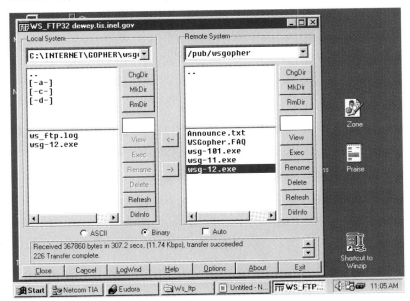

Figure 9.4 A typical FTP session with WS_FTP is made simple with this easy-to-use interface.

If you realize after connecting that you need to make a new folder on your computer for whatever you plan to download, click the MkDir button on the left side of the program. Type a folder name and click OK. Double-click the new folder name to open the folder.The file transfer itself is easy as pie:

1. Back on the right side, browse your way to the correct directory on the remote machine.
2. Open the folder on your local machine where you want to put the file.
3. Double-click the filename and wait for the file to download (or select it and click the left-pointing button between the two windows). WS_FTP will apprise you of its progress in downloading the file and will estimate the time remaining based on its rate of transfer.

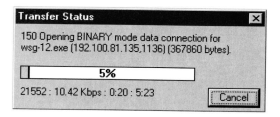

When the file is successfully downloaded, it will appear in the left window.

4. Click the Close button.
5. Click the Exit button.

Uploading Files with WS_FTP

To send a file to a remote machine (assuming you have permission—it simply won't work if you don't), the process is about the same. Find the file on your computer and double-click it in the left pane or select the filename and click the right-pointing button. As with downloading, click ASCII first if you're sending a text file (or check Auto to let WS_FTP deal with this for you).

Closing a Connection

When you're finished at a site, click the Close button at the bottom left (it will change back to a Connect button).

To quit the program, click the Exit button at the bottom right.

LOGGING INTO OTHER MACHINES WITH TELNET

Long before there were many Windows machines connected to the Internet, a protocol was devised for logging into remote machines from anywhere on the Net—Telnet (not telenet, which is something different entirely). This protocol was designed primarily to work with UNIX machines (along with VMS and others), and it grants a character-based connection only, meaning you won't be able to run someone else's Windows from your machine. There are resources out there on the Net—such as library catalogs and unique information services—that are only, or primarily, available via Telnet.

The Built-In Telnet Program

Windows comes with a perfectly decent Telnet client, called Telnet, naturally enough, in the Windows folder. To run it, double-click the Telnet icon in the Windows folder or select Start | Run, type **telnet** in the Open box, and click OK.

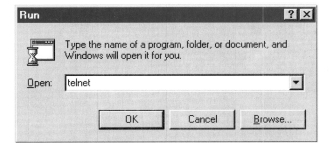

Figure 9.5 shows part of what appears in my Telnet window when I connect to fedworld.gov (it doesn't require a password, though many sites do).

SHORTCUT

You can also drag a file from a Windows folder into the right pane of the WS_FTP program to upload it to a remote site.

SHORTCUT

*If you know the address of the site you want to connect to, you can type **telnet** site.name in the Open box of the Run dialog box to run Telnet and connect to that site directly.*

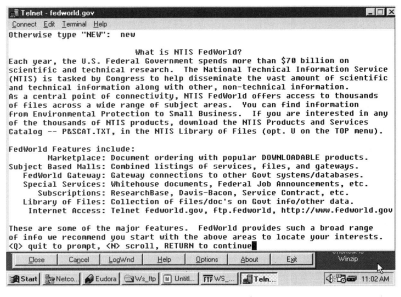

Figure 9.5 All kinds of information and documents related to the U.S. Federal Government can be found at the fedworld.gov telnet site.

When you're finished at a site, select Connect | Disconnect (notice that Telnet remembers the last few sites you visited).

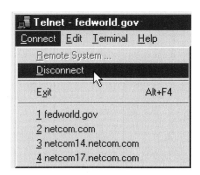

Entering a Site to Connect to

If you run Telnet without specifying a site in the command line, or if you want to connect to another site, select Connect | Remote System (or choose one of your last four sites).

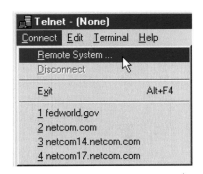

In the Connect dialog box, enter an Internet address in the Host Name box and, if you've been told one, a port number in the Port box. Telnet will keep track of old entries and allow you to select them from drop-down list boxes.

habits & strategies

*If you can't figure out how to navigate a program you've connected to via Telnet, try typing **h** or **?** (and ENTER, if nothing happens at first), to get help information for the program.*

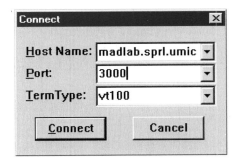

When the connection is made, you'll usually have to log into a remote account with a username and password. When in doubt, try logging in as "guest." Most programs that use the Telnet interface are menu-driven, meaning that you spend most of the time typing letters and numbers (sometimes followed by ENTER, sometimes not) to select items from menus.

Figure 9.6 shows a weather report for San Francisco from the madlab.sprl.umich.edu weather telnet site.

netiquette

It's best to log off from any service you've connected to before closing a Telnet connection, only because the site at the other end might spin its wheels for a while before it notices you're no longer there.

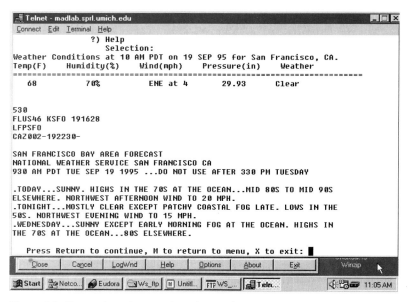

Figure 9.6 Better than the weather channel? Up-to-date weather information via Telnet.

If you disconnect from a site from a prompt or if the remote site "hangs up" on you for any reason, Telnet will let you know that the connection has been lost.

Plugging Telnet into Your Web Browser

Web pages can contain links to Telnet sites as easily as any other kind of link (the protocol, naturally enough, is telnet://). But most Web browsers nowadays are not themselves Telnet programs. They "shop the work out" to real Telnet programs, launched externally. For you to be able to follow such links, you have to tell your Web browser what program to launch.

To do so in Netscape, select Options | Preferences and click the Applications and Directories tab. Then type **telnet** in the Telnet Application box and click OK (see Figure 9.7).

Preferences ☒

| Styles | Fonts | Colors | Mail and News | Cache and Network |

Applications and Directories | Images and Security | Proxies | Helper Apps |

┌ Supporting Applications ─────────────────────────────────────┐

Telnet Application: `telnet` Browse...

TN3270 Application: Browse...

View Source: Browse...

└──┘

┌ Directories ───┐

Temporary Directory: `C:\TEMP`

Bookmark File: `C:\Program Files\Netscape\Navigator\Bookmark.ht` Browse...

└──┘

OK | Cancel | Apply | Help

Figure 9.7 If you tell Netscape about your Telnet program, it will launch it automatically whenever you click on a Telnet link.

ONE FROM COLUMN A: GOPHER MENUS

Before there was the Web, Gopher was the brave new face of the Internet. Gopher organizes connections (mostly using the FTP protocol) into menus, or directory listings, with plain-English names, so that you can browse the Net just by choosing items off of menus. In some ways, it's very similar to the Web concept except without all the page formatting and hyperlinks. Just as all the contents and resources of the Internet that can be reached with a Web browser can be said to be "on the World Wide Web," similarly, all the Internet resources than can be reached with a Gopher client are said to constitute Gopherspace.

A newer development of the Gopher protocol is GopherVR, a "graphical" (rather than menu-driven) Gopher space, organized with virtual reality technology.

For that reason, any Web browser makes a perfectly good Gopher client as well. (Yes, Gopher is another client-server protocol.) Needless to say, there are advantages to using a real Gopher program also. To some extent, though, the Web has superseded much of the role of Gopherspace, since it can offer menus, just as Gopher does, but additional context as well.

Using a Web Browser as a Gopher Client

To connect to a Gopher site with a Web browser, either click a hyperlink leading to such a site, or type the site's URL into your Location window.

Your browser will display a page called Gopher Menu featuring documents, folders, and links to search programs (see Figure 9.8).

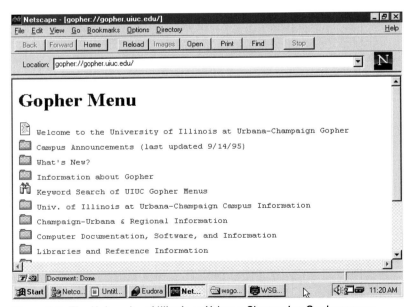

Figure 9.8 The University of Illinois at Urbana-Champaign Gopher menu. Each of those folders contain menus of their own. Text documents will be displayed in the Gopher window. Other documents can be downloaded.

To see the contents of a folder, click on its name. If you click on a search link (in Netscape, shown as a binoculars icon), you'll be prompted to enter a keyword and then will be shown a new menu with the results of your search. If you click on a file, your browser will offer to download it, unless it's in a format your browser knows how to display or open. If you click on a text file, it will be displayed in the browser window (see Figure 9.9).

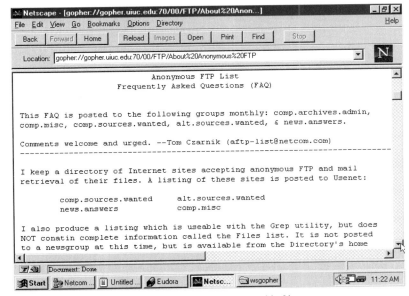

Figure 9.9 A FAQ about anonymous FTP displayed in Netscape

To continue browsing, click the Back button.

Gopher with a Gopher Client Program

As with FTP clients, one of the advantages of a full-fledged Gopher program such as WSGopher is that it comes with a preloaded set of worthy Gopher sites. You can download WSGopher from the dewey.tis.inel.gov FTP site in the /pub/wsgopher directory (as demonstrated in the WS_FTP section). Get the latest version of the self-extracting compressed file (it will have a filename of the form wsg-??.exe). Save it in or move it to its own folder and double-click it to uncompress it.

Wsgopher

To run WSGopher, double-click the Wsgopher icon.

The Gopher window appears, WSGopher connects to its home Gopher (something like a Web browser's home page), and it displays the first menu in a child window (see Figure 9.10).

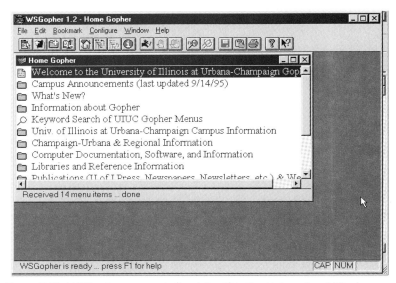

Figure 9.10 WSGopher connects (by default) to the University of Illinois at Urbana-Champaign Gopher, the same one shown in a Web browser in Figure 9.8.

To open a folder or view or download a file, double-click it. WSGopher will open a new window for each new menu or file you connect to. Most Gopher menus have an "Other Gopher Servers" or "All the Gopher Servers in the World" entry, so that you can work your way around the Net. Figure 9.11 shows a route taken to a U.C. Berkeley Gopher (yes, most—but not all—of the Gopher sites are at universities).

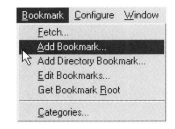

Gopher programs also use the term *bookmark* to refer to saved locations on the Net. To visit one of the stored locations, click the first button on the toolbar. The Fetch a Stored Bookmark dialog box will appear, showing a list of categories on the left side. Click one to see the bookmarked items in that category (see Figure 9.12). Double-click an item to connect to it.

As with the Web, if you arrive at an interesting Gopher menu that you might want to revisit in the future, select Bookmark | Add Bookmark. A dialog box called *Select category to save bookmark in* will appear. Choose a category and then click OK (see Figure 9.13).

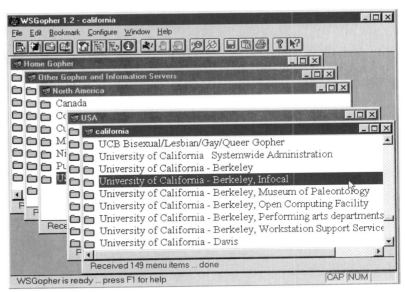

Figure 9.11 Looking for a Gopher at Berkeley, I found my way to a list of all the Gopher servers, then hunted through geographical choices to find California.

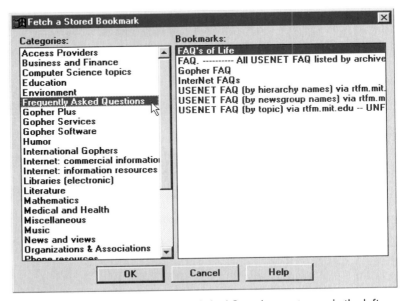

Figure 9.12 Choosing the Frequently Asked Questions category in the left pane reveals Gopher items related to FAQs on the right side of the Fetch a Stored Bookmark dialog box.

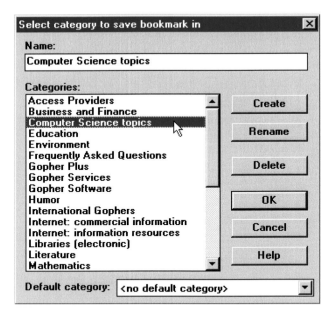

Figure 9.13 Saving a Gopher bookmark in the Computer Science category

There are other useful commands on the menus and toolbars (such as one that shows information about the current Gopher menu, one that enables you to change your Home Gopher, and so on). Explore the various options when you have the time.

SEARCHING FOR SITES

All the tools described in this chapter work well enough when you know where you're going. Often enough, someone will e-mail or tell you about an interesting site on the Net, and that's just fine. But sometimes you're going to have to go out there and find your own information. The Internet is changing constantly and there's no single directory, or table of contents, or index of the Net. There are, however, many serious and parallel efforts to organize the contents of the Net and keep on top of the changes.

Chapter 10 tells you a number of different ways you can search the Net for specific topics, and Chapter 11 points you toward some sites that will be useful or informative for a busy person learning about the Internet and using Windows 95. The last chapter shows you how to create your own Web page.

CHAPTER 10

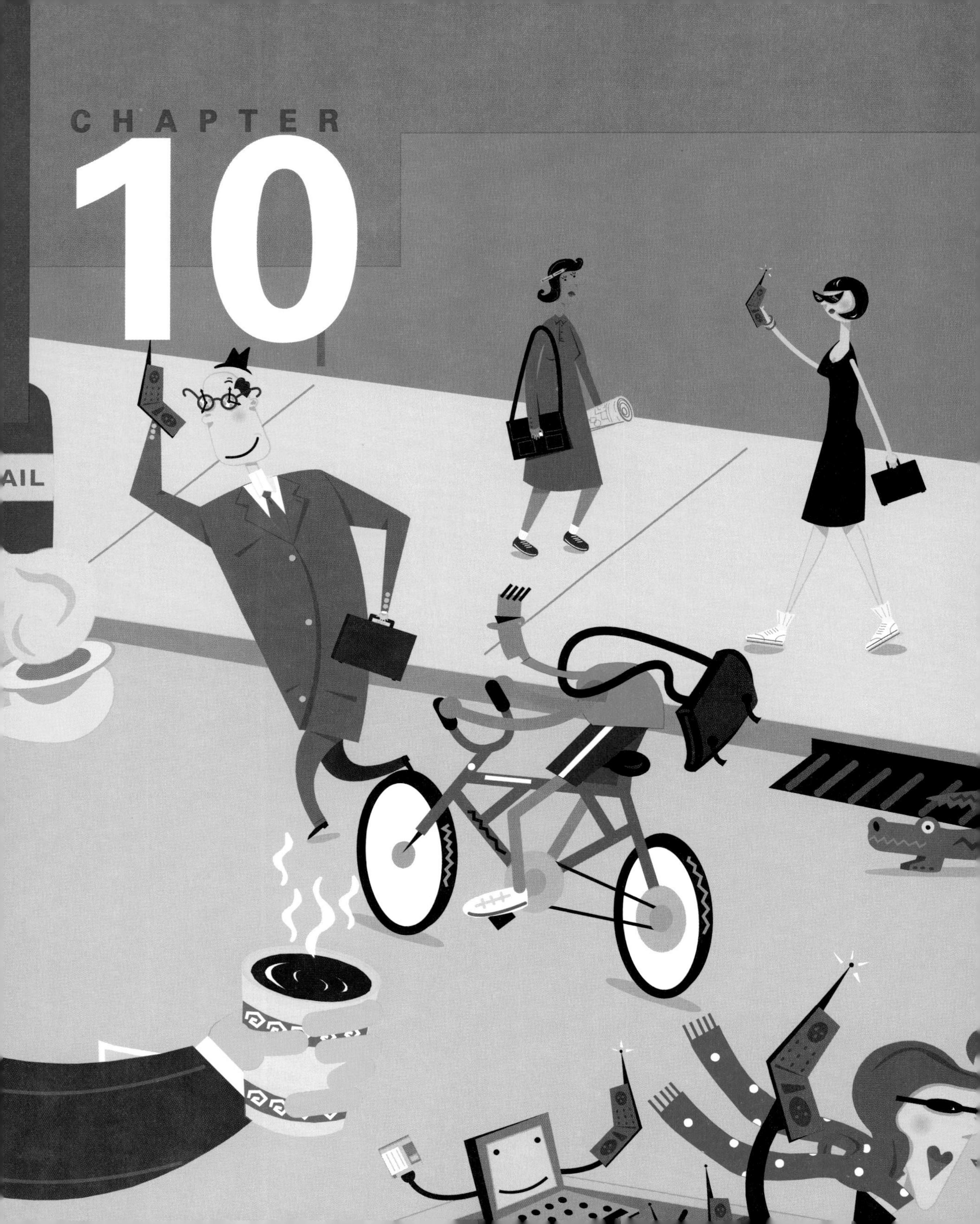

Searching the Net

FAST FORWARD

LOOK FOR INFORMATION IN DIRECTORIES ➤ *p 199*

Visit any of the Web pages listed in Table 10.1 to track down information organized by topic.

SEARCH FOR INFORMATION WITH SEARCH ENGINES ➤ *pp 200-204*

Perform keyword searches at:

- http://home.netscape.com/home/internet-search.html
- http://www2.infoseek.com/
- http://lycos.cs.cmu.edu/
- http://webcrawler.com/
- http://www.cs.colorado.edu/home/mcbryan/WWWW.html
- http://inktomi.berkeley.edu/query.html

HUNT FOR E-MAIL ADDRESSES ➤ *pp 207-210*

- Send mail to mailserv@ds.internic.net, leave the subject line blank, don't include your signature, and type the words **whois *name*** on a line by themselves.
- Telnet to bruno.cs.colorado.edu, log in as netfind, type **2**, and then enter the name to search for.
- Send e-mail to kis@cnri.reston.va.us or netaddress@ sol.bucknell.edu with no subject and no signature and the words **query *firstname lastname*** on a line by themselves.
- Send a message to mail-server@rtfm.mit.edu with no subject, and the words ***send* usenet-addresses/ *name*** on a line by themselves.

DejaNews query form

search for : scuba|

search - clear form - ? - 🏠

SEARCH USENET ARTICLES ➤ *pp 211-212*

1. Point your Web browser at http://dejanews.com.
2. When you arrive at the DejaNews home page, click the SEARCH link.
3. Type a word (or words) to search for in the "search for" box.
4. Click the search button.
5. Click the subject of any found article to read it.

As you've probably noticed by now, the Internet (not to mention the Web) is a nebulous, amorphous, constantly changing, regularly shifting blob of a network. Fortunately, there are brave souls out there working hard to make it comprehensible, as well as searchable. So when you're looking for information on a rare disease, or you're planning to go scuba diving in South America, or you're looking for a new job, try searching the Net using some of the methods described in this chapter. I'll point you toward some useful directory pages on the Web, show a few of the most useful Web and Internet search tools, run down some of the methods you can use to look for individual e-mail addresses, and show you a Web page from which you can search Usenet articles.

habits & strategies

Make some bookmarks for these sites, since you'll probably want to visit more than once.

NET DIRECTORIES

The directory pages shown in Table 10.1 overlap in many ways and often even point to each other, but if you want to hunt around for a topic and then find resources on the Net related to it, then starting with any of these directories is a good way to go. Figure 10.1 shows the home page of the Whole Internet Catalog, one of my favorite directories. It's the online equivalent (although updated more frequently, of course) of the classic book by the same title.

SEARCHING THE WEB FOR TOPICS

The next step in trying to find information on the Web is to perform a search using one of the many search engines available out there. Actually, there are several different senses in which you can search on the Web. For example, with any Web browser, you can search the text of the current page. This can be useful with very long pages.

SHORTCUT

In Netscape, press CTRL-F to search the current page.

Directory Name	Web Address
WWW Virtual Library, Subject Catalogue	http://www.w3.org/hypertext/DataSources/bySubject/Overview.html
WWW Virtual Library, by access method	http://www.w3.org/hypertext/DataSources/ByAccess.html
Whole Internet Catalog	http://gnn.com/wic/
Global Network Navigator	http://gnn.com/GNNhome.html
NCSA What's New	http://www.ncsa.uiuc.edu/SDG/Software/Mosaic/Docs/whats-new.html
Netscape What's New	http://home.netscape.com/home/whats-new.html
Internet Resources Meta-Index	http://www.ncsa.uiuc.edu/SDG/Software/Mosaic/MetaIndex.html
The Mother-of-all BBS	http://www.cs.colorado.edu/homes/mcbryan/public_html/bb/summary.html
The InterNIC InfoGuide	http://www.internic.net/infoguide.html
The Magellan Internet Directory	http://www.mckinley.com/
Point	http://pointcom.com/
The JumpStation	http://www.stir.ac.uk/jsbin/js
Scott Yanoff's Internet Services List	http://www.w3.org/hypertext/DataSources/Yanoff.html

Table 10.1 Some of the best directory pages on the Web

CAUTION

Because the information on the Net ages so quickly, often the pages you find from a search will already have been moved or changed. Try using several search engines to perform as thorough a search as possible.

You will also sometimes encounter pages with a notice saying "This is a searchable index." Pages that say this have been designed in such a way that if you type a keyword (or words) into the provided box and press ENTER, you'll be given back whatever matching information is available.

Finally, you'll encounter pages, such as those outlined in the next few sections, that are really front ends for databases, and often give you more control over your search than just entering a word or two. These pages usually have full-fledged forms on them, with most of the features you probably associate with dialog boxes (list boxes, check boxes, and so on). You fill out just as much of the form as is necessary and then click a button to submit your form and await results. Some databases have just the titles of documents stored; others have entire documents or abstracts with key words.

There are certain small, common words that you can't search for because they show up too often (words such as "is," "and," "the"). These words are sometimes called stop words or buzz words.

If you're running a different Web browser, you can still get to this page by going directly to http:// home.netscape.com/home/ internetsearch.html.

SHORTCUTS

You can also go directly to InfoSeek's home page to submit searches or explore their listings of Cool Sites (http://www.infoseek.com/).

Go directly to Lycos at http://lycos.cs.cmu.edu/.

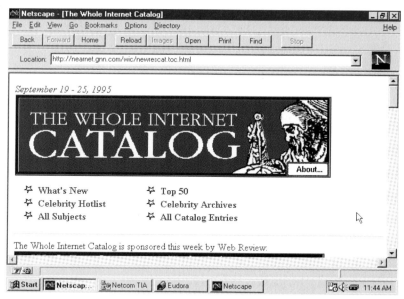

Figure 10.1 The Whole Internet Catalog is a thorough but discriminating listing of resources on the Net.

Netscape's Internet Search Page

One quick doorway to a number of useful search engines is Netscape's Internet Search page. To get there, select Directory | Internet Search.

InfoSeek

The Internet Search page incorporates a front end for the InfoSeek search engine. Type a word in the box and click the Run Query button (see Figure 10.2). InfoSeek won't search for words shorter than three letters. Put quotation marks around numerals.

InfoSeek will return a page with links to the first 10 Web sites it found that matched your keyword (see Figure 10.3).

Lycos

Another search engine linked from Netscape's Internet Search page is Lycos. Enter keywords in the box provided and click the Search button. Lycos returns a page full of links that match your query as closely as possible (see Figure 10.4).

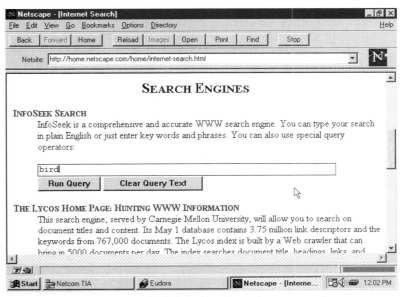

Figure 10.2 Type a word and click the Run Query button to perform an InfoSeek search from Netscape's Internet Search page.

You can often get more exact search results by searching for two or more words. Also, try more than one search engine, as their results differ substantially.

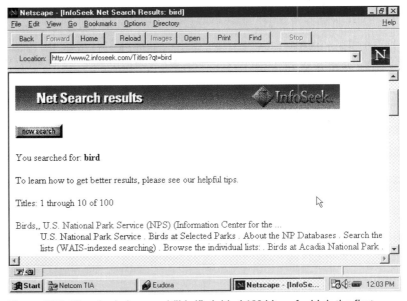

Figure 10.3 The single keyword "bird" yielded 100 hits, of which the first 10 are displayed on this page. Perhaps a more specific word (such as "hummingbird") might return a shorter list.

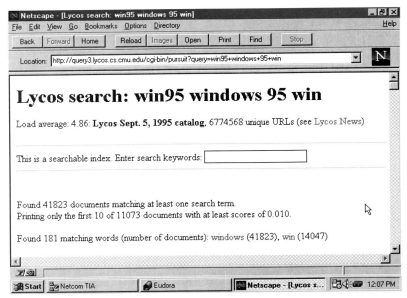

Figure 10.4 I entered the search words "win95 windows 95 win" to cover all my bases looking for Windows 95 information on the Net. Lycos scores hits based on how closely they match your criteria (that is, how many of your search words are found in the document, and how near they are to each other).

SHORTCUT

Go directly to WebCrawler at http://webcrawler.com/.

WWWW has an elaborate format with several list boxes enabling you to control your query in complex and subtle ways. For the most part, though, you can enter a simple keyword search as with the other engines.

WebCrawler

Yet another search front end linked from Netscape's Internet Search is WebCrawler. As with the others, enter a keyword in the box and click the Search button. You can also select from the drop-down lists to require that the returned pages match all or some of the keywords or to limit the number of pages to search for. (Naturally, the more pages you want to search the longer the search takes.) WebCrawler returns a very straightforward page of links (see Figure 10.5).

WebCrawler doesn't weight its results, so you can't tell which documents most closely match your search words. It also offers minimal context for each page it returns (that is, just the name of the page and a link to it, without any of the contents of the page).

WWWW

The World Wide Web Worm is another worthy search engine, but it happens not to be linked from Netscape's page. To get there, point your browser at http://www.cs.colorado.edu/home/mcbryan/WWWW.html.

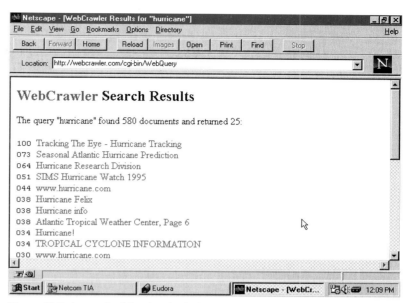

Figure 10.5 I searched for the single keyword "hurricane" with WebCrawler and got back these pages in return.

WWWW returns a page telling you how long the search took and offering a list of matching links (see Figure 10.6).

Inktomi

The newest, largest, and possibly fastest searchable index of the Web is called Inktomi. To get there, point your Web browser at http://inktomi.berkeley.edu/query.html. Enter your search word(s) in the Query Words box and then click the Search! button. Inktomi quickly returns a list of sites, weighted by how closely they match your search words (see Figure 10.7).

Security Warnings

Sometimes, when you click a button to submit a form, Netscape will display a warning dialog box to tell you that your transmission is not "secure."

If all you're doing is querying a search index, as in all the preceding examples, then there's nothing to worry about and you can go ahead and click Continue. This warning box is a side-effect of Netscape's proprietary security system, and you can happily ignore it most of the time (click Continue).

CAUTION

If you're trying to buy something over the Web and you're about to send your credit card number and expiration date, then you should cancel (especially if you are the type to tear up your credit card carbons).

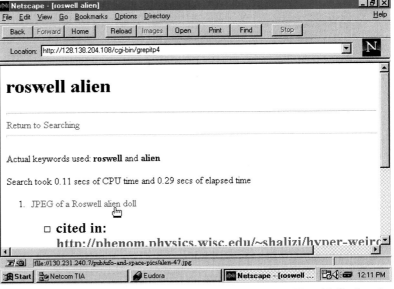

Figure 10.6 I searched with WWWW for the words "Roswell" and "alien" and found this link to an image (it turned out to be out of date and moved, though).

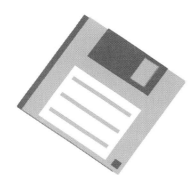

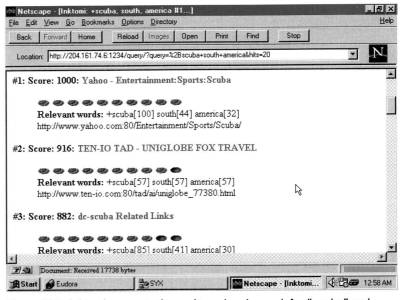

Figure 10.7 Inktomi suggests these sites when I search for "scuba" and "South America."

SEARCHING FOR GOPHER SERVERS AND FTP SITES

FTP and Gopher are explained in Chapter 9.

As FTP and Gopher sites proliferated on the Net, some protocols were developed for indexing the servers and making searchable lists of sites available. The system for searching FTP sites for files is called Archie. The system for searching Gopher menus for topics is called Veronica. (There was another experimental method called Jughead—I can't explain the Archie Comics mania in the naming of these protocols.) You can often find the front end for Veronica searches on main Gopher server menus (often near or at the bottom of the list). Both Archie and Veronica can also be accessed via Web gateways.

netiquette

Try not to perform Archie or Gopher searches during the busiest times of the workday.

To attempt an Archie or Veronica search from the Web, point your browser at the Internet Resources Meta-Index (http://www.ncsa. uiuc.edu/SDG/Software/Mosaic/MetaIndex.html).

Gopher Searches

To search for Gopher sites, scroll about halfway down the list (see Figure 10.8). You'll find information about how to compose Veronica queries by following the Veronica link. Eventually your search will yield up a Gopher menu, assembled on the fly.

Archie Searches

On the same Meta-Index page, under FTP, there are two front ends for Archie searches.

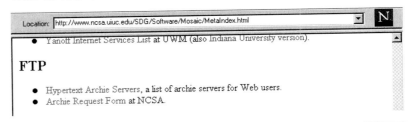

Location: http://www.ncsa.uiuc.edu/SDG/Software/Mosaic/MetaIndex.html

- Yanoff Internet Services List at UWM (also Indiana University version).

FTP

- Hypertext Archie Servers, a list of archie servers for Web users.
- Archie Request Form at NCSA.

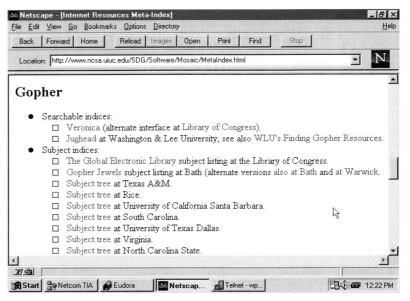

Figure 10.8 The Internet Resources Meta-Index features links to some Gopher indexes. Click any of these links to search for Gopher menus containing keywords.

Archie servers are notoriously flaky, so it may take several tries at different times of the day to get back any useful results. The form you fill out allows you to specify a case-sensitive search (but assumes you want "case-insensitive" unless you change it), control the impact on the rest of the Net, choose an Archie server (choose one geographically near you—or try servers in Japan and the UK, which seem to be the most reliable), and restrict the number of results (the fewer the faster—you can always redo a search). Figure 10.9 shows my search for FTP sites with information or files related to VRML.

netiquette

Choose at least a "Nice" impact on other users, so as not to hog network resources. The "nicer" an impact you choose, the lower the priority of your query when "competing" with other network resources.

Figure 10.9 I'm searching for "vrml," without regard to case, with a "Nice" impact on other users, at the nearest Archie server, with a maximum number of 10 returned documents.

Your results page will contain links both to FTP servers and to specific documents stored on them. If you have trouble using the Web Archie interface, try telnetting to any of the Archie servers and entering your search directly.

SEARCHING FOR E-MAIL ADDRESSES

Aside from looking for information, you might also want to see if someone you know is reachable by e-mail. As with the rest of the Net, e-mail addresses exist pretty much in chaos, so there's no single definitive list of e-mail addresses anywhere, but there are several imperfect avenues you can try.

Whois

One way to look for e-mail addresses is to perform a Whois search. There are several ways you can do this. You can telnet to a Whois server, such as whois.internic.net (for a list of available servers,

habits & strategies

If you're looking for the e-mail address of someone affiliated with a university, try the campus Gopher and/or Web pages, which might well have a listing of addresses. This is true for some big corporations as well.

go to ftp://sipb.mit.edu/pub/whois/whois-servers.list). You shouldn't have to log in. Type

```
whois name
```

at the prompt and press ENTER.

You can also perform a Whois search by mail. Send your message to mailserv@ds.internic.net, leave the subject line blank, don't include your signature, and type the words **whois *name*** on a line by themselves.

```
         To: mailserv@ds.internic.net
       From: xian@netcom.com (Christian Crumlish)
    Subject:
         Cc:
        Bcc:
Attachments:

whois crumlish
```

The server will query a series of Whois servers and send you its results (see Figure 10.10).

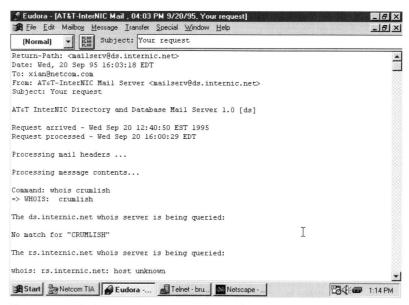

Figure 10.10   As I usually find, there is apparently no record of my e-mail address at any of the databases. The ds.internic.net server says "No Match for 'Crumlish'."

Netfind

Another source for e-mail addresses is Netfind. To perform such a search, you must telnet to a Netfind server and log in as netfind. One server to try is bruno.cs.colorado.edu.

Once you connect, type **2** to perform a search. Then type the name of the person you want to search for and press ENTER.

Netfind lists alternate servers on its opening screen, so copy and paste the list to a file somewhere if you want to try other servers or if the one at Colorado is busy

Knowbot

Knowbot is a variation on the Whois system. Knowbot searches are expressed in the form

```
query firstname lastname
```

To perform a Knowbot search, telnet to info.cnri.reston.va.us (port 185) or send e-mail to kis@cnri.reston.va.us or netaddress@sol.bucknell.edu with no subject and no signature and the words **query firstname lastname** on a line by themselves.

```
             To: kis@cnri.reston.va.us
           From: xian@netcom.com (Christian Crumlish)
        Subject:
             Cc:
            Bcc:
    Attachments:

    query christian crumlish
```

Like the Whois mail server, the Knowbot returns the results of a series of Whois searches to your mailbox.

```
kis input >> query christian crumlish

Connected to KIS server (V1.0). Copyright CNRI 1990. All Rights Reserved.

Trying whois at ds.internic.net...

The ds.internic.net whois server is being queried:

No match for "CRUMLISH and CHRISTIAN"
```

Once again, the question of my existence on the Net remains unconfirmed by a robotic e-mail directory service, in this case the Knowbot.

Usenet Addresses

The kind souls at the RTFM archive site at MIT regularly compile a database of e-mail addresses and associated real names, culled from Usenet postings. Although you can log into the FTP site at rtfm.mit.edu and go to /pub/usenet-addresses/directory, the site is so popular and so busy that you might have trouble getting in. The lower-impact way to get your results is to send a message to mail-server@rtfm.mit.edu with no subject, and the words

```
send usenet-addresses/name
```

on a line by themselves. The mail-server at the FTP site will search its lists for the name you send and return its results (see Figure 10.11).

Figure 10.11 Hallelujah! I exist after all, thanks to my occasional posts to Usenet newsgroups. Looks like there's another long-lost cousin out there as well.

Postmaster@

When all else fails, if you know the domain and host portion of someone's e-mail address (if, for example, you know where they work or go to school), try sending e-mail to postmaster@*that.address* and asking politely for the person's e-mail address.

SEARCHING THE VAST USENET FEED

Finding something on Usenet is difficult. For one thing, articles expire after a while. For another, you can never keep up with all the newsgroups where a given topic might be discussed. Fortunately, there's a fast, powerful index of Usenet available on the Web, called DejaNews.

To search Usenet articles for a topic, point your Web browser at http://dejanews.com. Click the SEARCH link. Type a word (or words) to search for in the "search for" box.

If you want to filter the articles by author, date, or newsgroup (you can use wildcards), click "create a query filter" in the options section. On the page that appears, enter a newsgroup, a date range, and or an author name, and then click the Submit Filter button.

If you want to see articles that match all the words, and not just any one of them, click AND next to "Default operator."

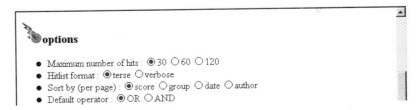

When you're ready, click the Search button. DejaNews will quickly generate a list of articles matching your search criteria (see Figure 10.12).

Click the subject of an article to read it or click the author's name to see a profile of that author's Usenet postings.

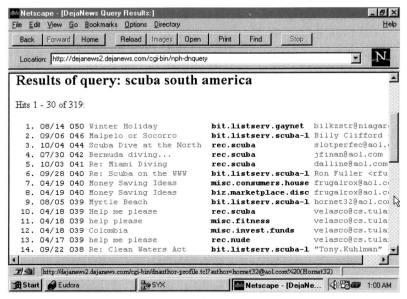

Figure 10.12 I searched for "scuba" AND "South America" and got these articles.

SOME STARTING POINTS AND HELP WITH ORGANIZING SITES

Chapter 11 discusses some additional sites to check out (beyond the directory sites listed in this chapter), and gives you a way to organize your Netscape bookmarks with a plug-in program called SmartMarks. Chapter 12 will help you get your feet wet creating your own Web page.

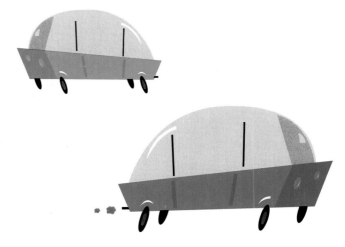

CAFÉ

MAIL

Places to Go, Things to See

215

FAST FORWARD

Go to: http://syx.com/x/busy/

VISIT THE BUSY PERSON'S LINKS ➤ *p 217*
Point your browser at http://syx.com/x/busy/ to get quick access
to the Web pages mentioned in this chapter (and throughout
the book).

FOR INTERNET INFORMATION ➤ *p 217*
Try EFF's Guide to the Internet at
http://www.eff.org/papers/eegtti/eegttitop.html.

TimesFax
FROM THE PAGES OF
The New York Times

FOR THE LATEST NEWS ➤ *p 219*
Visit the FAX edition of the *New York Times* at
http://www.nytimesfax.com/.

In the spirit of Thomas Jefferson,

TO CHECK UP ON THE U.S. CONGRESS ➤ *pp 220-221*
Lobby the Thomas Web site at http://thomas.loc.gov.

Keywords: world wide web

Generate Anagrams

TO COME UP WITH
ANAGRAMS OF ANY WORD ➤ *p 221*
Enter the word into the Anagram Generator at
http://csugrad.cs.vt.edu/~eburke/anagrams.html.

Netscape SmartMarks
Current version: 1.0 (1.3MB)

DOWNLOAD SMARTMARKS ➤ *pp 221-223*
To help organize your bookmarks, try out Netscape's SmartMarks
add-in. To download it and install it, follow these steps:
  1. Point your Web browser at http://home.netscape.com/.
  2. Click Netscape Now!, choose Windows 95, and click
     Netscape SmartMarks.
  3. Indicate where you're located on the clickable map, and then
     click a download link.
  4. Save the file (Sm10r2.exe) to a temporary folder and then
     double-click it to uncompress it.
  5. Run the Setup program to install SmartMarks.

CAUTION

The Web changes rapidly. Some of these sites may have moved by the time you get to them. If you can't find a listed site, try searching for it by name (see Chapter 10), or visit the Busy Person's Links page, which will stay up to date.

SHORTCUT

These and other sites are all listed on the Busy Person's Links page (http://syx.com/x/busy/), which I maintain.

You now have all the skills you need to explore and make use of the Internet. You know how to browse the Web and, if you've read Chapter 10, you know how to search it and where to look for directories. The Web changes fast, so it's difficult to single out specific sites you definitely should visit. Nevertheless, I've put together a small set of sites you might find interesting. After that, you're on your own.

WEB SITES WORTH VISITING

The Web sites in this section are divided into several categories. First, we discuss sites related to the Internet, especially in the context of Windows 95. Next you'll get miscellaneous Windows 95 resources and tips. Then we list up-to-date news sources, so you can keep up with breaking news efficiently. There's a section on business and financial topics, one for U.S. Government sites, and finally, for if you ever do get a breather from work, a section on entertainment and complete wastes of time.

Of course, the sites recommended here are a tiny fraction of the interesting and worthwhile sites on the Web today, and there are new sites cropping up all the time.

Internet

The following table offers some Internet information sites.

Site Name	Web Address
Internet Society	http://www.isoc.org/
EFF's Guide to the Internet	http://www.eff.org/papers/ eegtti/eegttitop.html
Zen and the Art of the Internet	http://oingomth.uwc.edu/ inetguide/Zen/zen-1.0_toc.html
The Consummate Winsock Apps List	http://cwsapps.texas.net/
Windows Internet Software	ftp://ftp.lightside.com/lightside/win/ InternetSoftware/

Site Name	Web Address
Windows Win 95 TCP/IP PPP Internet Connectivity Instructions	http://www.erv.com/ w95_ppp.htm
The Windows95 TCP/IP Setup FAQ	http://www.aa.net/~pcd/ slp95faq.html
NetWatch	http://www.pulver.com/netwatch/

Window 95 and Shareware

Listed here are some Windows 95 sites, such as the one shown in Figure 11.1, that don't specifically deal with the Internet, and some sources for Windows 95 shareware.

Site Name	Web Address
NetEx Windows 95 Software Archive and Discussion Forums	http://www.netex.net/w95/
Win95-L Windows 95 FAQ	http://walden.mo.net/~rymabry/ 95winfaq.html
Windows 95 FAQ	http://www.process.com/win95/ win95faq.htm

Figure 11.1 NetEx Windows 95 Software Archive and Discussion Forums

Site Name	Web Address
Windows 95 Tips, Tricks, and Undocumented Features	http://www.netex.net/w95/tips.html
Windows 95 Annoyances	http://ocf.berkeley.edu/~daaron/win95ann.html
Windows 95 Links	http://uptown.turnpike.net/W/Windows95/95links.htm
Virtual Software Library	http://vsl.cnet.com/

News

Get a cup of coffee and check out some of these news links. Many of these, such as Mercury Center (Figure 11.2), are offshoots of major newspapers.

Site Name	Web Address
Newspaper and Current Periodical Room	http://lcweb.loc.gov/global/ncp/ncp.html
Mercury Center	http://www.sjmercury.com/home.htm
NY Times Syndicate	http://nytsyn.com/
NY Times FAX	http://nytimesfax.com/
NandO.net	http://www.nando.net/
The Gate	http://www.sfgate.com/

Figure 11.2 The Mercury Center, the online child of the *San Jose Mercury News*

Business and Finance

Check out some of these sites for business, personal finance, and home office information. If you're like me, you may find yourself visiting the Investing for the Perplexed site frequently.

Site Name	Web Address
FinanceNet	http://www.financenet.gov/
Investor Web	http://www.inverstorweb.com/iwebhome.htm
Taxing Times	http://www.scubed.com:8001/tax/tax.html
FDIC Gopher	gopher://fdic.sura.net:71/
SEC Edgar Database	http://town.hall.org/cgi-bin/srch-edgar
Electronic Credit Repair Kit	http://www.priment.com/~kielsky/credit.html
America's Job Bank	http://www.ajb.dni.us/
Home-Based Wealth	http://www.we.com/hbw/
Investing for the Perplexed	http://www.inch.com/~robertny/invest/menu.html
Wall Street Journal Money and Investing	http://update.wsj.com/
Small Business Resource Center	http://www.webcom.com/~seaquest/

U.S. Government

Slowly but surely the U.S. Government is getting its act together and taking it on the Net. Three of the most useful sites are listed here.

Site Name	Web Address
The White House	http://www.whitehouse.gov/
Thomas	http://thomas.loc.gov/
Library of Congress	http://loc.gov/

Thomas, shown in Figure 11.3, is the Web site of the U.S. Congress. From its home page, you can download the full text of any bill pending on Capitol Hill, read the entire congressional record, track the progress of specific bills, search or read the constitution, reach your representative by e-mail (if she has an address), and much, much more.

Entertainment and Complete Wastes of Time

You can't be busy all the time. Pretend you're working and check out these sites. Use the Internet Movie Database to solve all your movie-related arguments here.

Site Name	Web Address
Internet Movie Database	http://www.msstate.edu/movies/welcome.html/
50 Greatest Conspiracies	http://www.webcom.com:80/~conspire/
biancaTroll productions	http://bianca.com/btp/index.html
Useless WWW Page	http://www.primus.com/staff/paulp/useless.html
The net.legends FAQ	gopher://dixie.aiss.uiuc.edu:6969/11/urban.legends/net.legends.FAQ
eye.NET — The stupid net.coverage media awards	http://www.interlog.com/eye/News/Eyenet/Awards.html
The Urban Legends gopher site	gopher://dixie.aiss.uiuc.edu:6969/11/urban.legends
Anagram generator	http://csugrad.cs.vt.edu/~eburke/anagrams.html

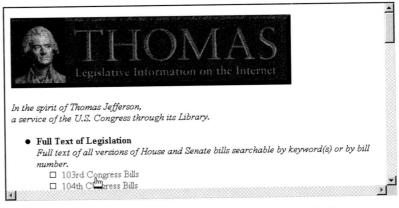

Figure 11.3 The home page of Thomas, the Web site of the U.S. Congress, named for Thomas Jefferson, who believed that the political process should be open to the people.

ORGANIZING BOOKMARKS WITH NETSCAPE SMARTMARKS

If your bookmark list starts getting unwieldy, you might want to install an external bookmark-manager program, such as Netscape Smartmrarks. SmartMarks enables you to organize bookmarks hierarchically into folders and to track interesting Web sites for changes, so you'll know if anything's new before you visit. SmartMarks is a Netscape add-in (like Netscape Chat, discussed in Chapter 8), so it will not work with other Web browsers.

Downloading and Installing SmartMarks

Point Netscape at its own home page (click the N icon in the upper-right or select Directory | Netscape's Home), and click the button that says Netscape Now!

On the page that appears, select Windows 95 or NT. Then click the Netscape SmartMarks link on the next page.

Finally, click on the map to indicate where you are located. You'll arrive at a page with a list of sites from which you can download SmartMarks. Read the installation instructions and license agreement. Then click on a download link. When Netscape asks you what to do with the file, click Save and save it in a temporary folder. If you have trouble connecting to one of the sites, try another until you get through.

Netscape SmartMarks
Current version: 1.0 (1.3MB)

To install SmartMarks, close all running programs, open the temporary folder, and double-click the Sm10r2 icon. The program files will extract themselves. When they're done, double-click Setup to install the program. Follow the installation instructions (they're as normal as can be).

Using SmartMarks

Once you install SmartMarks, it runs automatically every time you start Netscape Navigator (see Figure 11.4).

SmartMarks comes with a large set of bookmarks already organized into folders that, aside from being green, look just like Windows Explorer folders. To go to any of the bookmarked sites, just open a folder and double-click the name of the bookmark in the right pane of the SmartMarks window.

On the Navigator side of things, the Bookmarks menu will be replaced by a SmartMarks menu. Instead of Add Bookmark, you now have Add SmartMark (same shortcut, CTRL-A); instead of View Bookmarks, you now have View SmartMarks (same shortcut, CTRL-B), which switches to or opens the SmartMarks window. You also get a new option, File SmartMark, for adding a bookmark not to your main Bookmark menu but to a SmartMarks folder.

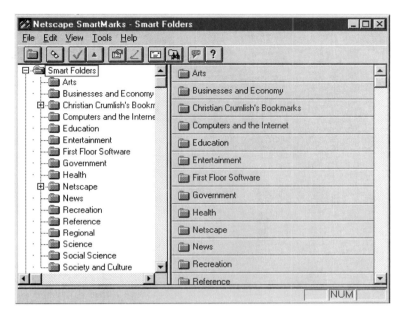

Figure 11.4 SmartMarks comes up automatically when you run Navigator. Maximize the window to see all the folders on the left. SmartMarks comes preloaded with a large number of bookmarks, organized into categories, but you can add to them.

When you select Bookmark | File SmartMark, the Add SmartMark dialog box appears. Choose a folder to save the page in, and check "Notify me when this page changes," if you want SmartMarks to watch the page for you. Then click OK.

HAPPY SURFING!

As soon as I wrote the above heading, I thought of my friend Trevor, who's a writer and a surfer (he compiled *The Surfin'ary*, a dictionary of surf slang). He shudders every time he hears someone call sitting at a computer clicking a mouse "surfing." Still, it's already idiomatic, so there's no fighting it. You now have everything you need to get the most out of the Web (and the rest of the Internet).

For those interested in taking their involvement a step further, Chapter 12 introduces the basics of Web page design and creation. It's a lot easier than you might think.

PRIORITY!

A Web Design Primer

WonderWeb

With Links Up the Wazoo!

But first, you'll want to read all of our press releases for the last fifteen years.

```
sample - Notepad
File  Edit  Search  Help
<HTML>
<HEAD>
<TITLE>A Sample HTML Document</TITLE>
</HEAD>
<BODY>

<H1>This is a Sample HTML Document</H1>
```

Featuring Overuse of Formatting!

Yes, that's right, *emphasis* left and right. Silly stuff. Applied *tackily*, without regard for GOOD DESIGN.

That calls for a *clean break*.

```
<HTML><HEAD><TITLE>The Amazing
<H1>WonderWeb</H1>
<H2>With Links Up the Wazoo!</H
But first, you'll want to read
<A HREF="press.html">press rele
for the last fifteen years.
</BODY></HTML>
```

FAST FORWARD

PLAN A WEB SITE ➤ *p 229*
- Organize your source documents
- Consider possible interlinks
- Create a folder hierarchy
- Design your home page
- Plan for future growth

ALL HTML DOCUMENTS ➤ *pp 231-232*
1. Start with <HTML>.
2. Have a head that starts with <HEAD>, has a title enclosed between <TITLE> and </TITLE>, and ends with </HEAD>.
3. Have a body that starts with <BODY> and ends with </BODY>.
4. End with </HTML>.

FORMAT A WEB PAGE ➤ *pp 234-235*
Insert HTML tags, mostly in pairs surrounding affected text, such as:
- <H1></H1> through <H6></H6> for headings
- <P> before new paragraphs
- <B></B>, <I></I>, and <U></U> for bold, italics, and underline
- <HR> for a horizontal line
-
 for a line break without starting a new paragraph

EMBED A HYPERTEXT LINK ➤ *pp 236-237*
Insert an HTML anchor tag, usually of the form
<A HREF="*filename*">Active text</A>.

DOWNLOAD INTERNET ASSISTANT FOR WORD ➤ *pp 237-238*

1. Point your Web browser at Microsoft's Download page for Internet Assistant—http://www.microsoft.com/msoffice/freestuf/MSWord/download/ia/ia95/chcklist.htm (if that page doesn't work, go to the main Microsoft page—http://www.microsoft.com/—and then follow links for Software, MS Office, and Internet Assistant).
2. Click download Internet Assistant now.
3. Save the wordia2 (or wordia2b) file in a temporary folder.
4. Double-click wordia2 to install Internet Assistant.

FORMAT WEB DOCUMENTS WITH INTERNET ASSISTANT ➤ *pp 238-240*

- Click the Title button to assign a title.
- Assign heading levels with the Style drop-down list in the Formatting toolbar.
- Format text with any of the normal formatting buttons that remain on the toolbars.
- Click the Insert Picture button to insert a picture.
- Click the Hyperlink button to insert a hypertext link.

PROMOTE A WEB SITE ➤ *pp 240-241*

- Communicate with the creators of similar or like-minded Web sites and offer to exchange hyperlinks.
- Visit the directory and search engine sites listed in Chapter 10 and register your Web site at each.

Just when you've gotten yourself an e-mail address and begun to explore the World Wide Web, you learn that there's another level of status on the Internet these days— having your own home page. The best-known open secret on the Net is that making a home page is easy. It's just a matter of putting together a text file and adding a few *tags*.

Meanwhile everybody and their brothers' companies are setting up sites on the Web, ranging from flimsy storefront mail-drops to complex interactive worlds. You may be too busy to design and build a complicated Web site, but you'd be surprised how easy it is to put together a few simple pages, or make information from your department available to everyone within your company, or promote a project.

AN OVERVIEW OF WEB PUBLISHING

Suddenly, the World Wide Web has opened up an entirely new avenue of publishing, one that avoids much of the costly overhead of print publishing and which is open to anyone—or at least anyone with access to a Web server. A Web server is a program that delivers requested pages to Web client programs (browsers).

A Web publication (or site) consists of a home page, all the Web pages that are linked from the home page, all the pages linked from *those* pages, and so on. You should always be able to return to a site's home page from any page at the site. Not every page need be linked directly from the home page, but the essence of a well-designed Web publication is the organization of the links.

If a site is intended for the Internet public at large, its documents should be placed in a directory at a Web server. If it is only intended for the internal use of some company or department, then the documents can be placed on any computer volume accessible to the entire local network. (This means that within a specific network, you can serve up Web pages without a server.) If you get your Internet access from a

CAUTION

I can't go into the details of installing and running a Web server in this short space. If you're about to try your first Web publishing project, request access to a server at your organization or one run by your Internet service provider. Some providers will offer Web server access separate from e-mail accounts.

I'll cover just the basics of Web-site creation in this chapter—but enough for a busy person!

If you organize your documents with a judicious structure of folders, you'll find it easy to maintain and update the site in the future.

service provider, ask if you also get access to a Web server as part of your account.

PLANNING A WEB SITE

Here are the steps to follow in designing a Web site:

1. Clarify the relationships between documents and organize a structure for the pages at the Web site.
2. Design, write, and format the documents.
3. Assemble the publication by incorporating hyperlinks.
4. Promote the Web site to its intended audience.
5. Maintain the site with regular updates.

If you are basing a Web site on existing documents, or a mixture of existing documents and newly created ones, assemble all your source documents and plan a folder hierarchy that reflects how they relate to each other.

Think carefully about how you want your documents to link to each other. This is likely the part of Web design you are least familiar with. Linking documents in sequence is often a good place to start, but don't overlook the potential for creative and flexible cross-linking of documents. Often a single document will refer to several others. Each of those references can be an active link. You can link to specific parts of documents too.

Try to plan for potential future growth of your site. The Web is not a static medium. An orphaned site quickly becomes stale and out of date. Think about what areas of the site might end up being expanded upon or replaced. If you anticipate future changes, such as updated statistics or newer publications, they'll be much easier to implement when the time comes.

WEB PAGES EXPLAINED

So what exactly is a Web page? It's an HTML document, with the extension .htm on Windows computers (.html everywhere else). But what's an HTML document? It's really just a plain text document with special "tags," each of which starts and ends with angle brackets. Look at an HTML file and you'll be <I>surprised</I> at how easy it is to read.

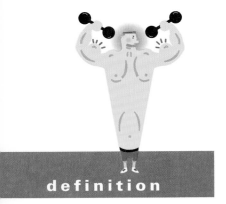

definition

HTML: *Hypertext markup language. A system of tags used to describe hypertext documents that consist mainly of text, formatting instructions, and hypertext links.*

To see the source of a Web page in Internet Explorer, right-click on an empty part of the document in the window and select View Source from the menu that pops up.

A Little HTML Never Hurt Anyone

In most browsers, it's very easy to take a look at the underlying HTML document that's the source for the displayed Web page. In Netscape, and most Web browsers, the command is View | Source.

The HTML source will appear in a new window (see Figure 12.1).

The fastest way to learn about HTML is to look at source files for interesting pages.

Word Processing Add-Ins

I'll explain the basics of HTML here, but you don't have to read about it if you don't want to. There are more and more tools appearing

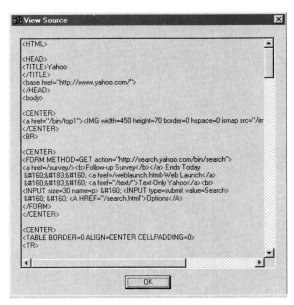

Figure 12.1 The source HTML file underlying Yahoo's home page. You can select and copy sample HTML from such a window and paste it into a new file.

*With most browsers, you can assign a text editor such as Notepad as your Web source viewer (in Netscape, Options | Preferences, Applications and Directories tab, type **notepad** in the View Source box), if you prefer.*

on the Net that enable users to create Web documents without having to know much about the underlying HTML tags. Generally, they let you create and format a document normally, and then perform a conversion for you. At the very least, they can automate the insertion of tags and hypertext links.

I'll explain one such tool, the Word for Windows add-in called Internet Assistant, later in this chapter. (See "Creating Web Pages with Internet Assistant for Word.")

HTML Document Layout

All HTML documents must start with <HTML> and end with </HTML>. Between those codes are two sections, the head and the body, marked at start and end by <HEAD></HEAD> and <BODY></BODY>, respectively. The only tag inside the head of the document that you need to know about is the title tag (<TITLE>*the title goes here* </TITLE>). Figure 12.2 shows a diagram of a basic Web document.

The actual HTML file based on the diagram in Figure 12.2 is shown in Figure 12.3.

Interpreted and displayed by a Web browser, the sample document appears as in Figure 12.4.

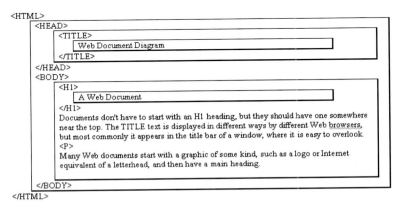

Figure 12.2 A conceptual diagram of a basic Web document

For additional HTML resources,

check Yahoo or any of the

directories or search engines

described in Chapter 10.

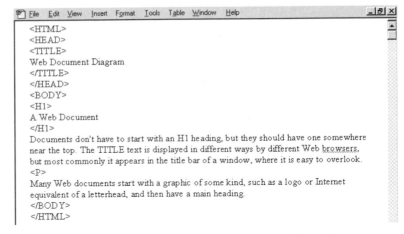

Figure 12.3 The actual HTML Web document without all those boxes

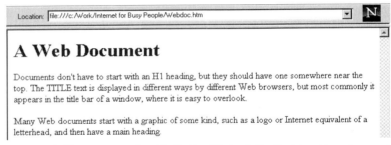

Figure 12.4 Now you see the title (in the title bar), the first-level heading, and the two paragraphs, as displayed in Netscape.

Online Reference Material

If you want to learn more about HTML, visit some of the reference sites on the Web shown in Table 12.1.

CREATING WEB PAGES WITH A TEXT EDITOR

Skip ahead to "Creating Web Pages with Internet Assistant for Word" if you have a Web-publishing program, tool, or add-in. This section explains how to create Web pages with a simple, raw text editor, such as Notepad.

Whenever possible, try to reuse

existing Web documents, copying

them and rewriting them, to save

yourself the tedium of entering

the basic tags over and over.

Site Name	Web Address
Hypertext Markup Language (HTML)	http://www.w3.org/hypertext/WWW/MarkUp/
HTML Quick Reference	http://kuhttp.cc.ukans.edu/lynx_help/HTML_quick.html
Style Guide for Online Hypertext	http://www.w3.org/hypertext WWW/Provider/Style/Overview.html
How Do They Do That with HTML?	http://www.nashville.net/~carl/htmlguide/index.html
HTML Tutorial	http://fire.clarkson.edu/doc/html/htut.html
WWW & HTML Developer's JumpStation	http://oneworld.wa.com/htmldev/devpage/dev-page.html

Table 12.1 Online HTML references (how do you think I learned all this?)

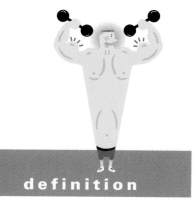

definition

RTF: *Rich Text Format. A Microsoft text-based format designed to retain formatting information for file transfers between incompatible systems or formats.*

Converting Old Documents

If you plan to reuse or adapt existing documents, you'll need to save them as text files or in RTF format. If you save them as plain text (ASCII) files, you'll have to insert all the HTML tags manually. If you convert them to RTF, you can then use an RTF to HTML converter to get them at least part of the way into shape.

For an RTF converter, point your Web browser at ftp://ftp.cray.com/src/WWWstuff/RTF/rtftohtml_overview.html, the "rtftohtml" home page (see Figure 12.5).

Or, for a Word *and* RTF converter, try http://www.stattech.com.au/, the Stat Tech home page, where you can download a free version of E-Publish.

Writing the Text

A big part of the job, as with the creation of any document, is the writing of the text. Do it in a word processor and save it as a text file with line breaks, or type it in your text editor if you prefer. As with any formal document, do the writing and the formatting in different stages, so that each job is done thoroughly.

Because Web browsers ignore line breaks in HTML documents, press ENTER any time you want to make your HTML document clear and easy to read or edit.

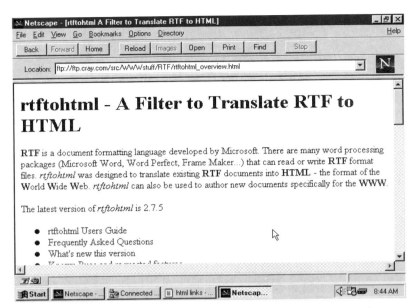

Figure 12.5 The rtftohtml home page. rtftohtml is a free filter you can download from the Web.

netiquette

To suggest the intention of formatting (such as emphasis) instead of the result (such as boldface or italics), use the EM and STRONG tags, which leave the details of emphasis up to each individual browser.

Formatting a Web Page

All the formatting tags you incorporate into your document will go between the <BODY> and </BODY> tags. Most tags go before and after the text they affect, in pairs. Table 12.2 shows a basic set of tags you'll probably want to use. For elaborate documents, consult with an actual designer. Putting together a graceful document is harder than it looks. At the very least, pick up a simple design reference.

Figure 12.6 shows a sample Web document illustrating the results of various formatting tags, when displayed in Netscape.

Numbered and bulleted lists can be "nested," one inside of another, to create subordinate list levels, but be careful not to "cross" the tags.

Purpose	Tag
First- through sixth-level heading	<H1></H1>,...,<H6></H6>
New paragraph	<P>
Line break, same paragraph	
Horizontal line	<HR>
Bold, Italic, Underline	<B></B>,<I></I>,<U></U>
Emphasis, Strong emphasis	<EM></EM>,<STRONG></STRONG>
Equal-width text (as made by a typewriter)	<TT></TT>
Start, end numbered list	<OL></OL>
Numbered list item (don't type the number)	<LI>
Start, end bulleted list	<DL></DL>
Bulleted list item	<LI>
Start, end definition list	<DL></DL>
Definition term	<DT>
Definition	<DD>

Table 12.2 Some of the most common formatting tags

CAUTION

Pictures take longer to download than text and consume more hard-disk space, so use judiciously. Keep art small and reuse graphical elements, as they'll only have to be down-loaded once.

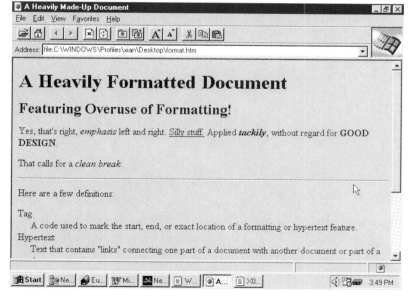

Figure 12.6 No paragon of design, this sample page illustrates some common formatting effects.

Inserting Graphic Images

Don't overlook the mixed-media potential of the World Wide Web. A big part of the sudden popularization of the Internet centered on the Web is the simple fact that Web pages can display pictures (on most Web browsers). Web sites with illustrations and effective use of graphics are much more inviting and communicative than the text-only world that the Internet has only recently emerged from.

The two widely recognized graphics image file formats on the Web are GIF (extension .gif, CompuServe's Graphics Image File format) and JPEG (extension .jpg, the Internet standard promulgated by the Joint Photographics Experts Group). GIFs are still the most widely displayed, but JPEGs are almost universally recognized now, and can be compressed to much smaller sizes, albeit with some trade-off in image quality.

The basic tag for inserting a figure is <IMG SRC="*filename*" ALT="*text*">, where *text* is alternative text to be displayed by non-graphical browsers and browsers with image loading turned off. To learn more about the <IMG> tag, view the source of some pages using illustrations in ways that you'd like to.

Inserting Hypertext Links

The bottom line of the Web is its "hypertext" nature. The real genius of hypertext is that it hides the baroque Internet addressing protocols that are so clumsy to discuss and learn about. Sure, you still have to type in some URLs, but even those are getting easier. (For example, you can visit my Web site by just typing **syx.com** in Netscape or Internet Explorer.) Most of the time, though, navigating the Internet can be as simple as pointing to the name of something you want to see or hear and clicking your mouse.

There's the rub. To make your own Web site, it's up to you to plan and insert the hypertext links. The HTML tag used for hypertext links is <A>, the anchor tag; you can use it in any of the ways shown in Table 12.3.

Some programs can only display pictures in external viewers, but most can now place them in-line as part of the page design.

habits & strategies

Make sure documents are in the same hierarchical relationship where you're creating them as they will be when and if moved.

Link Element	Anchor Tag
Clickable hypertext link pointing to another HTML document or other type of file (such as a sound file or movie file)	<A HREF=" *filename* ">*Active text*</A>
Hypertext link pointing to a named anchor in this same document	<A HREF=" *#name* ">*Active text*</A>
Link pointing to a named anchor in another HTML document	<A HREF=" *filename#name* ">*Active text*</A>
Named anchor point	<A NAME=" *name* ">*Active text*</A>
Combined link and anchor	<A HREF=" *filename*" NAME=" *name* ">*Active text*</A>
Clickable image link	<A HREF=" *filename* "><IMG SRC=" *button-graphic* "></A>

Table 12.3 Hypertext link anchor tags

Finishing the Web Document

When you're finished working on your document (for now), save it, but not as a text file (or it will get the .txt extension). Instead, specify "All Files" in the Save as Type box in the Save As dialog box of your text editor, and type a filename with the .htm extension at the end.

File name:	sample.htm		Save
Save as type:	Text Documents	▼	Cancel
	Text Documents		
	All Files [*.*]		

CREATING WEB PAGES WITH INTERNET ASSISTANT FOR WORD

Microsoft's Internet Assistant for Word converts HTML documents to Word documents and vice versa. It also has a bunch of toolbar

items and menu choices useful for Web page design. First you need to download the add-in. Follow these steps:

1. Point your Web browser at Microsoft's Download page for Internet Assistant—http://www.microsoft.com/msoffice/freestuf/MSWord/download/ia/ia95/chcklist.htm (if that page doesn't work, go to the main Microsoft page—http://www.microsoft.com/—and then follow links for Software, MS Office, and Internet Assistant).
2. Click "download Internet Assistant now."
3. Save the wordia2 (or wordia2b) file in a temporary folder.
4. Double-click the wordia2 icon to install Internet Assistant.

Converting Old Documents

If you plan to base a Web page on an existing document, open the document. Select File | Templates. In the Templates and Add-ins dialog box, type **html**, check Automatically Update Document Styles, and click OK. Then save the document (Word should automatically suggest "HTML Document" in the Save as Type box). I suggest using a one-word name for each Web document.

Creating a Web Document from Scratch

Starting a Web document even without a model Word document is also simple. Select File | New. Select the HTML template and click OK. Save the new file as an HTML document right away.

Formatting the Web Page

Type the text of the document as you normally would. You won't be inserting HTML tags directly. Instead you'll use Word's normal formatting commands, such as the Bold, Italic, and Underline buttons on the Formatting toolbar, along with special HTML-related commands on the toolbars and styles that are equivalent to HTML tags.

Switch to Web Browse view
Go back
Go forward
Horizontal rule
Title
Hyperlink
Bookmark
Picture

For example, to make a line of text into a first-level heading, select the text and then select the Heading 1,H1 style in the Style drop-down list box in the Formatting toolbar.

Impose HTML formatting for which Word has direct equivalents, such as numbered and bulleted lists, with the normal Word toolbar or menu commands.

This is technically not part of formatting, but to assign the document's title (usually displayed in a Web browser's title bar), click the Title button, type a title, and click OK.

Inserting Graphic Images

To insert a picture into a Web document, first place all your graphics files in a single folder. Then click the Picture button and select a picture from the dialog box that appears. Then click OK.

Inserting Hypertext Links

Internet Assistant takes the tedium out of inserting links. First, select the word (or graphic) you want to serve as the launching point to the linked destination. Then click the Hyperlink button.

This brings up the HyperLink <A> dialog box (<A> is the HTML tag for links; it stands for anchor).

If you want to link to a local document, select it from the To Local Document tab of the HyperLink dialog box. (The box lists both .doc and .htm files. If you link to a regular Word file, only people using Word as a Web browser will be able to read it.) To link to an address on the Web, click the To URL tab. Then type the address in the box or select from a list of URLs you've already typed (see Figure 12.7).

To link to a specific section of a document, choose the To Bookmark tab and choose a document and bookmark name.

If you plan to link to a bookmark within a document, make sure the bookmark exists (or create it), before you try to link to it. (There's a Bookmark button on te HTML toolbar.)

Figure 12.7 Type the URL exactly to link to another document on the Web (Internet Assistant will remember all the URLs you type and allow you to reuse them easily).

Then click OK. The text that activates the link will appear underlined and blue (as is typical of links when displayed in Web browsers).

Finishing the Web Document

When the document is completed (for now), save it as an HTML document. You can test the links by clicking the Switch to Web Browse View button.

Clicking any link should take you to the linked document or bookmark. Use the Back and Forward buttons in the toolbar to retrace your path.

PROMOTING A WEB SITE

What if you built a storefront and no one came? It can happen on the Web, where sure, you can set up shop on prime real-estate, directly across from Time/Warner's megaWebsite, but you'll still see no visitors unless you promote your site. Without promotion, a public Web site is a lonely voice, crying in the wilderness. To start with, if there are Web sites for related issues or interests, send their webmasters e-mail and offer to exchange links.

Then visit all the directory and search engine sites mentioned in Chapter 10 and submit the URL of your Web site to each one. (They all have pages where you can fill out forms to submit Web addresses.)

netiquette

Don't spam (send multiple or unwelcome messages to) mailing lists or newsgroups to promote your site. Be careful to keep commercial messages out of noncommercial areas.

ADVANCED WEB DESIGN

There are more possibilities in Web design, although not all of the latest advances have yet been implemented in standard HTML rules or in all or even most browsers. Some advanced elements have become almost commonplace. It's a full-time job keeping up with Web design developments, so focus on content first, presentation second, and embellishment last. Here's a list of advanced Web design features you might want to explore: alignment commands, tables, borderless figures, gutter space around figures, transparent figure backgrounds, faster-seeming interlaced images, background patterns on pages, background colors on pages, customized text colors, variably sized text, pages that load themselves, style sheets with recommended settings.

WELCOME TO THE NET

No matter what degree of participation you choose or how much information you avail yourself of, you're now part of a global community, vital and growing. There's no reason why the Internet has to eat up all your time and energy. You now know enough to make productive use of the Net, avail yourself of its vast resources, and avoid entangling yourself in technical distractions.

For a shortcut to all of the Web pages referred to in this book, be sure to visit the Busy Person's Links (http://syx.com/x/busy/). See you on the Net!

habits & strategies

When you think you're ready for prime time, ask some friends or colleagues to "beta test" your pages to look for typos, broken links, or other potential problems. Try to find people who will be using different browsers or types of computers to test your pages.

MAIL

What Kind of Connection?

If you're poking around back here in this part of the book, then you're probably confused about something. No problem. I'm here to help.

First of all, you may already be connected to the Internet, to some degree. If you are, your first step is to identify the type of connection you have. If you don't yet have an Internet connection, I can help you figure out what kind of connection you want and how to find a service provider offering that type of hook-up.

Even if you have direct access to the Internet at work, you might still want to dial up your network from home, or connect to a private service provider, perhaps to make personal or business use of the Internet that might not be appropriate to conduct over your work connection.

Direct access means working on a computer that is itself either directly connected to the Internet or connected to a smaller network that is itself directly connected to the Internet. *Dialing up* a network means using a modem and a computer to connect to a network over phone lines. An *Internet service provider* (ISP) is a private company that specializes in providing Internet access, especially dial-up access for individuals. A direct network connection to the Internet is usually the fastest, but if your access comes by virtue of your employment at a company or membership in a department or organization, then your participation in the Internet may be limited by your capacity as a representative of your organization. Many companies consider it improper for you to conduct personal business over a company Internet connection, although personal e-mail is usually permitted, within reason, to the same extent that personal phone calls are.

Once you've found some service providers, grilled them thoroughly, and compared their services and prices, you'll still have to get your computer set up, so I'll cover those details, not only for Windows 95 but also for other versions of Windows (and even Macintosh systems). Oh, and the last thing I do in this appendix is explain what's required to set up a home page on the World Wide Web.

One final disclaimer: Yes, this stuff is boring. That's why we stuck it in the back of the book. I won't pretty anything up—I'll just tell you the details and move on.

AM I ALREADY CONNECTED TO THE INTERNET?

What does "on the Internet" mean? It depends. If all you're mainly interested in is e-mail, then any type of e-mail system that can send mail to and receive mail from Internet addresses is "on the Internet." If you want to be able to browse the Web, then you'll need either a direct network connection to the Internet or a dial-up connection.

Are You on a Network at Work, School, Prison, etc.?

If you use or have access to a computer that's part of a network and that network is connected in some way with the Internet, then you may be able to run a Web browser, for example, and your network will provide the Internet connection. This is often true at universities and larger corporations.

You might have to ask whoever maintains your network. If you don't have direct access to the Internet from a local network, jump ahead to "How Can I Get Connected to the Internet?". If you're not sure exactly what a network is or what it means for it to have a gateway to the Internet, read on.

What's a Network?

In most cases, the networks you encounter will be office-wide (Local Area Networks, LANs) or campus-wide (Metropolitan Area Networks, MANs). These are physically linked computers and other peripheral machines (such as printers), often with central "server" computers overseeing the traffic and functioning of the network. The largest type of network is called a Wide Area Network (WAN).

What's a Gateway?

A network can connect to other networks via cable or phone hook-ups, provided it has a gateway, usually composed of a piece of equipment and the software that controls it. For example, an e-mail gateway is the software that translates an e-mail message from its format on the local network to a more universal Internet format, before sending it over a physical piece of hardware (gate) to the Internet. (In this case, the Internet usually takes the form of a much larger network that itself has gates to larger networks still.)

Do You Subscribe to an Online Service (CompuServe, America Online, etc.?)

If you have an account at an online service, such as CompuServe, America Online, Prodigy, or the Microsoft Network, then you already have fairly complete access to the Internet, though you may have to learn some specific rules and methods that are particular to your service. They all offer technical support, although some are occasionally swamped with calls.

The most common model for Internet access from an online service is a local e-mail system with a gateway to the Internet, local discussion groups mixed in with Usenet newsgroups, and the capacity to run a separate Web browser (such as Netscape or Mosaic) when connected to the service. This last feature is not available from every provider. Some offer their own Web browsers as part of the overall service.

If your online service allows you to run a program such as Netscape when connected, then you most likely can run all the other programs discussed in this book, also while connected. You may be more comfortable, however, with the "interface" provided by your service, and therefore might not opt for Winsock-compatible programs, for the most part. (Appendix B covers connecting to and exploring the Microsoft Network.)

WHAT KIND OF CONNECTION DO I HAVE?

If you have a network connection (that is, you're on a network, and the network is connected to the Internet), then you shouldn't have to set up anything yourself (aside from specific programs, as explained throughout the book). Enjoy your network connection. If you want to dial-up to connect to your network and run graphical programs from a modem, then you'll be using a PPP (or SLIP). This requires configuring some software and possibly putting together a dial-up script. Windows 3.1 requires the most helper software and massaging to get going. Windows 95, Windows NT, and Macintosh are pretty easy to set up for PPP (or SLIP). You should be able to get technical support to do this.

By the way, *PPP* stands for *Point-to-Point Protocol,* and it's the preferable method for doing Internet traffic over a modem. *SLIP* stands for *Serial Line Internet Protocol,* and is nearly as good a method for the same thing. (PPP is faster and more efficient than SLIP.)

If you subscribe to an online service, make sure that you're getting "full Internet access." You shouldn't have to do any setup beyond installing their software. Here's the key question: Ask them if you have full PPP or SLIP access. If they say yes, then you can run any of the software mentioned in this book.

If you already have an Internet service provider, then you either have a PPP or SLIP account perfectly suited for all the instructions in this book, or you have a dial-up UNIX "shell" account. If the latter is the case, then you'll be using mostly different software than that described in this book (mainly a terminal/communications program on your personal computer and then a number of UNIX programs at the other end all in a character-only interface).

HOW CAN I GET CONNECTED TO THE INTERNET?

OK, now say you don't yet have Internet access. That means you need to find a *service provider*, which is a company that specializes in hooking up individuals to the Internet. If there are more than one in the local area, so much the better. Competition does wonders for Internet rates. You shouldn't have to spend more than $30 a month for a reasonable amount of Internet access, and you can spend closer to $20 in larger metropolitan areas.

Finding a Service Provider

Shop around before choosing a provider. Compare the rates of direct-access Internet service providers (ISPs), such as Netcom, Hooked, Portal, Pipeline, Crl, and so on, to online services such as AOL, MSN, CompuServe, Prodigy, etc. See if there is a Free-Net in your area (a public access network) or if any local universities are offering access. If you have to compromise more than you want on price for a provider, you can get an additional forwarding address with an e-mail forwarding company such as pobox.com (e-mail info@pobox.com or http://pobox.com on the Web) and give out the pobox address. Then you can move your provider when a better deal becomes available and not have to inform everyone you know or do business with that your address has changed. The pobox service costs $15 for 3 years.

Some people prefer to start exploring the Net through the more controlled environment of an online service. The big online services are often more expensive than ISPs, but they do offer additional content of their own, and in some regions their prices may be competitive. They also offer more hand-holding and all-in-one interfaces that can be easier to use, but limited.

If you can get or borrow Web access visit http://www.tagsys.com/Providers/index.html. You can enter your area code there and search for service providers who offer local-call access in your area. (This is essential to keeping your costs down.) Look in local newspapers and computer periodicals for other listings of providers.

What Questions to Ask

When you call up a service provider and tell them you're looking for access to the Internet, here are some specific questions to ask them.

- Will I have a PPP of SLIP connection, and can I use header compression?
- Will I be able to browse the Web (and see pictures), send and receive e-mail, subscribe to Usenet newsgroups, and so on?

- How busy are your modems? Will I ever have trouble getting through? When are the peak usage hours?
- Does the service provider include a disk of useful software (such as connection software, a Web browser, an FTP program, a mail reader, and so on) with the service?
- Will it be easy to set up? Will the provider or installation software do all the geek work (such as IP configuration)?
- What is the top dial-in modem speed? The top dial-in modem speed should be at least as fast as your modem—the slower modem in a connection controls the speed. Today, the fastest modems are 28.8 Kbps (kilobits per second), but 14.4Kbps modems are still standard. A provider that can handle only 9600 bps (bits per second) modems is woefully behind the times.
- Is there flat-rate access (a rate for unlimited time)?
- Is there a local dial-up number?
- Are there any hidden or extra charges?
- Are there any quotas or limits on disk storage, e-mail, or other Internet traffic?
- Does the provider offer the capacity to set up a home page on the World Wide Web?

Also, if you encounter people on the Internet with the domain name of a provider you're considering, ask them what they think of the service.

WHAT KINDS OF CONNECTIONS DO I WANT?

Your best bet is a direct PPP or SLIP account, or some other sort of account that is equivalent (such as a NetCruiser account from Netcom or a full Internet access account from MSN, both of which amount to full PPP access).

Your next best choice would be a UNIX "shell" account, but you'd want to obtain and install an "emulator" program, such as SLIrP or TIA, that will enable you to run most PPP software. You could run a mail program such as Eudora on a shell account without any special arrangements.

Lastly, an online service with partial Internet access or a service provider with their own unique interface (one that does not permit you to plug in standard programs), would be an adequate first step toward full Internet access.

SETTING UP DIFFERENT TYPES OF CONNECTIONS

Here are the essentials of setting up an Internet connection. You'll need to get specific details from your service provider, but most likely they'll offer the information and may possibly set up your software for you, saving you the trouble. If you get stuck anywhere, your provider can "walk you through" the problem and get you set up (some charge a premium for this sevice).

A Network with an Internet Gateway

Your network system administrator should be able to tell you either that you can simply go ahead and run Internet software such as Netscape and send Internet e-mail out from your network e-mail program, or that you'll have to set up a TCP/IP network connection or, for Windows 3.1, obtain a Winsock driver to enable Internet software to run. A Winsock driver enables a PC not connected to a network to send and receive TCP/IP packets. (Windows 95 comes with a Winsock driver.)

Setting up the TCP/IP will mainly entail typing certain numerical Internet addresses (your sysadmin can give you the addresses) into specific boxes, to indicate specific gateways and servers (see Figure A.1).

If you need to find a copy of Winsock to download, see the Winsock FAQ (http://papa.indstate.edu:8888/winsock-faq.html). Windows 95 comes with Winsock.

On a Macintosh, if you have system 7.5 or later, then you have the MacTCP control panel already installed on your computer. You'll have to purchase MacTCP from Apple for earlier versions of the Macintosh.

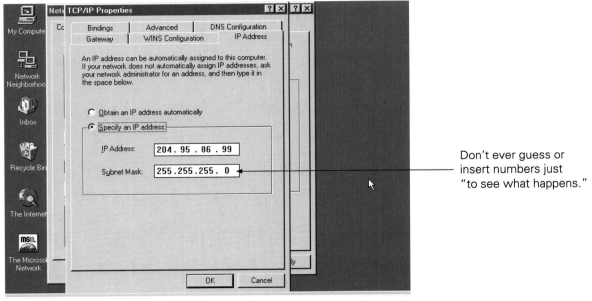

Don't ever guess or insert numbers just "to see what happens."

Figure A.1 In Windows 3.1, on a Mac, or on another type of computer, the specific program and dialog box may look different, but the type of information you have to supply remains the same.

Dial-up PPP or SLIP

To get a PPP or SLIP connection going, you need to have the same software and settings in place as are needed for a network connection. (That is, you'll need TCP/IP software running, and on Windows machines you'll need Winsock.) You'll also need a PPP or SLIP dial-up program to make and maintain your phone connection to the Internet. Windows 95 has built-in software for PPP (and you can get the SLIP driver from http://www.microsoft.com). For a Mac, you'll need InterSLIP (http://www.intercon.com/) or

MacPPP (http://www.compumedia.com:80/pub/Software/mac/MacPPP.sit.bin. For Macintosh Internet software, see Appendix C. For Windows 3.1, you'll need a third-party PPP or SLIP program, such as Chameleon Netmanage (http://www.netmanage.com) or Trumpet (http://www.trumpet. com.au/wsk/winsock.htm).

No matter what conglomeration of programs you're using to maintain your PPP (yes, or SLIP) connection, you'll need to tell it the correct modem settings and numerical Internet addresses, for nameservers, e-mail, and news.

Example Windows 95 Setup

So, for example, to set up a PPP account on Windows 95, start by double-clicking My Computer and then double-click the Dial-Up Networking folder. Then double-click the Make New Connection icon.

Type your provider's name in the corresponding box of the setup Wizard and then click the Next > button. Enter the phone number and then click Next > again. Make sure the information is correct and then click the Finish button. That's the easy part. Then right-click on the new connection icon that will appear in your Dial-Up Networking folder and select Properties.

In the dialog box that appears, click the Server Type button. Make sure PPP is chosen as the connection type. Click the TCP/IP Settings button. If your provider assigns you a new address every time you connect (you can ask this) make sure *Server assigned IP address* is checked. Otherwise, your provider should give you primary and secondary name server addresses and you should enter them in the boxes provided in this dialog box. Assuming that your provider can handle "header compression," also known as Van Jacobsen C/SLIP or C/PPP (it makes your connection faster, ask them), check *Use IP header compression*. Then click OK.

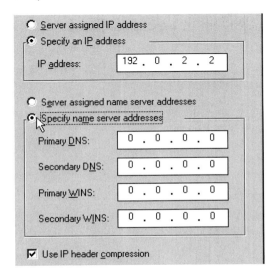

Then click OK twice to close the window.

To set up a direct network connection, you'll need the full host and domain name of your connection, addresses of DNS (Domain Name Server, don't worry about it) name servers, an IP (Internet Protocol, ditto) address and a "subnet mask," and one or more gateway addresses from your system administrator. Get the information together and select Start | Settings | Control Panel and then double-click the Network icon in the Control Panel window. Make sure the Configuration tab is selected and then click the TCP/IP choice in the box.

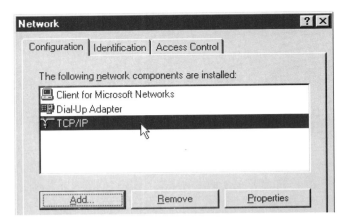

Click the Properties button. This brings up another dialog box. First click the DNS Configuration tab and enter the name of your host and the domain it's in (see Figure A.1). Then enter the DNS name server numbers in the spaces provided. Next click the IP Address tab and enter your IP address and subnet mask, if any. Finally, click the Gateway address tab and enter one or more gateway addresses. Don't worry about what any of this means. Click OK twice.

Online Service

Ask your online service whether the Internet access is only directly through the service's software (and gateways) or whether you can run Winsock client programs, such as a Web browser. If you can, then the software installation for the online service should also take care of your PPP setup. If not, the service's technical support should tell you what to do. If you sign up for MSN with full Internet access (see Appendix B), then your settings will all be taken care of automatically.

If you have both direct Internet access *and* an MSN account, MSN will "offer" to overwrite the address information of your other provider with MSN information. You can respectfully decline this advice if you don't want to go through the hassle of reentering your other provider's information later. MSN also overwrites a different version of Winsock.dll that CompuServe and other online services require as part of their full Internet access dial-up. If you have this problem with an online service, contact them for the remedy. They're well aware of this Microsoft "bug."

By the way, Windows 95's Plus! Pack also comes with a dial-up networking scripting tool for putting together a simple dial-up script, so you won't have to log in by hand every time.

All-in-One Interfaces

There are some Internet access providers that give you a single piece of software that can perform all of the Internet procedures for you. For some, you can still run external programs but for others you can't. Netcom's NetCruiser is all-in-one software that does permit the use of external client programs. To be sure, ask your provider if their software creates full PPP access (allows you to run Winsock programs). Either way, simply installing the software should take care of all your connection and setup requirements.

A Unix "Shell"

Setting up a UNIX account is easy, at least as far as your local computer is concerned. At the PC end, you have to run a terminal, or communications, program, such as HyperTerminal in Windows 95, Terminal in Windows 3.1, or Zterm or Microphone, or Versaterm on the Macintosh. (By the way, UNIX "shell" is often used as a synonym for "UNIX account," but it technically means the command-line interface.)

You need to tell your terminal program the phone number and type of modem connection to make (your provider will give you all this information), as well as what type of "terminal" to emulate, meaning what kind of old-fashioned computer screen your program will pretend to be. The most common choice is VT100.

Then when you dial your provider with your terminal program you'll encounter a login prompt where you'll enter your username and then your password. After this, it's the wonderful command-line driven world of UNIX. If you liked DOS, you're going to love UNIX! (Some commands, such as **cd**, are the same.)

Fortunately, the Eudora mail program is smart enough (and the Post-Office Protocol it uses is crafty enough) that you can still run Eudora (either the Mac or PC version) with this kind of account. Eudora itself can dial up your connection and download your mail. Your other option is to use Elm or Pine, both excellent UNIX mail programs, while still connected by the terminal program. To learn more about any UNIX program, type **man *program***, such as **man pine**, and press ENTER. This will display the program's manual pages on the screen (if there are any).

If you're a little more adventurous, you can obtain an "emulator" program that can simulate a PPP or SLIP account when running on your UNIX shell. Once you get a program like that installed, you can follow the instructions for a PPP installation on your personal computer (as explained earlier in this appendix). Two such programs worth checking out are SLIrP (http://www.blitzen.canberra.edu.au/slirp/) and TIA (http://marketplace.com/tia) as well as SLIrP/TIA FAQs and Related URLs (http://www.webcom.com/~llarrow/tiafaqs.html).

If you'd rather try to cope with the world of UNIX, there are many powerful Internet programs available on every UNIX network, including newsreaders such as Trn, Tin, and Nn; Irc; Ftp, and a more advanced program called Ncftp; Telnet; Gopher; and Web browsers such as Lynx and Www; along with many other programs. There are many Usenet newsgroups where you can get help with the world of UNIX. Search for newsgroups with "unix" and/or "wizards" in their names, or read the many excellent FAQs.

GETTING A HOME PAGE

Once it was enough to have an e-mail address to seem really "with-it" on the Internet. Nowadays that requires a home page as well, anything from a potential Who's Who entry or Dewar's-style profile of yourself to a billboard, storefront, or electronic edifice. Many service providers have gotten with the program and automatically offer you space on their Web server at least for a personal home page, if not for a commercial page. Most will charge you something extra for a commercial page. Many will also offer to set up your pages for you, but—as with all things—you should shop around first before deciding (or at least drop by http://syx.com first!).

If you have Internet access through a network, ask the administrator if the network has a Web server or plans to install one any time soon. If so, ask for space on it for a home page. If your service provider offers space on a server, make sure you're aware of any disk storage limits or traffic quotas. Overuse of the system may cost extra (read the fine print and be sure you understand it). You may also want to know whether you can have direct access to the server (and can, for example "ftp" your documents into place), or if you have only indirect access to the server and your provider has to approve and manually post any additions or changes.

Finally, if you are planning to do business on the Internet and particularly on the Web, you might want to look into establishing and reserving a domain name for your company. Yes, mcdonalds.com and ibm.com are already taken, but your company name may well still be available. Some service providers will help you set up a domain name and charge you for the service. Again, shop around. Many of the companies that specialize in Web publishing, design, and setup, such as my own, are also fully equipped to help you establish a domain name for a reasonable price.

MAIL

Basics of the Microsoft Network

Like most online services, from big-time international networks to small community bulletin boards, the Microsoft Network (MSN) offers two services: access to the Internet and access to MSN's own private content. If you value the content provided only on MSN (or another online service), then it might be worth paying more to receive that context. If you use an online service primarily for Internet access, be sure to compare the costs to direct-access Internet service providers. (See Appendix A for more on finding a service provider.)

For Windows 95 users, MSN is perfectly tailored to fit in with and operate smoothly with the operating system. Resources on MSN appear in folders inside windows, looking only slightly different from the folders and windows showing your hard disk and files. This appendix will tell you how to sign up for a free 10-hour trial on MSN, and how to connect to, navigate, and access the Internet through MSN. Like any good online environment, MSN is best learned and experienced online, not in the back of a book, but the information in this appendix will get you through the starting gate.

SIGNING UP FOR MSN

To sign up for the Microsoft Network, double-click the Set Up The Microsoft Network icon on your Windows 95 desktop. (It may also just say The Microsoft Network.) Or click Start | Run, type **signup**, and press ENTER.

A huge dialog box will appear, bragging about MSN. Click OK. You'll be asked for the first three digits of your phone number. Type them and press ENTER. In the complicated-looking dialog box that appears, click the Connect button. The signup program gets the text of MSN's current free trial offer and a list of local phone numbers. The dialog box will tell you that it's "Dialing..."; it will say when each part of the job is "(done)".

Finally, you'll reach a dialog box with three big buttons down its middle. Click the Details button at the bottom of the dialog box. You'll be shown the latest information about MSN. Assuming you're already planning to check it out, go ahead and click Close.

Next, click the Price button, to the right of the Details button. MSN displays the details of its 10 hour free trial offer. Read it and click Close. Now, it's time to work your way down the three big buttons in the middle of the dialog box.

Click the top button (Tell us your name and address). In the boxes provided, enter your name, address, and phone number, and then click OK. Click the middle button (Next, select a way to pay). Then choose a credit card and enter your bank name, card number, expiration date, and your name as it appears on the card. Then click OK. Click the bottom button (Then, please read the rules). Scroll through and read the rules of MSN. Warning! Thick legalese ahead. When you've satisfied your curiosity and assured yourself of your rights and responsibilities, click the I Agree button.

Then click the Join Now button at the bottom of the MSN dialog box, to the left of the Details button. Then click the Connect button (the dialog box now looks more or less like the first time you connected to get the info and phone numbers). After connecting, type a Member ID (BobJones, melville, J.Smith)—this will be the username portion of your e-mail address; you'll be BobJones@msn.com or melville@msn.com, etc.—and a password. The password has to be at least six characters long. Write it down where no one will intercept it. Then click OK.

CONNECTING TO MSN

Any time you want to connect to MSN (also called logging in or signing in), double-click The Microsoft Network icon on your desktop. The Sign In dialog box appears. Your member ID should already appear in the box, as should your password. If not, type the password now. Also, click the Remember my password check box so you won't have to type it again in the future. Then click Connect (see Figure B.1).

If you already have an Internet setup on your computer, MSN will offer to replace your settings with settings for MSN. If you don't, skip ahead.

- If you don't want to change anything just yet, click No.
- If you know for sure that you don't want to change your Internet settings, check Don't ask this question in the future and then click No.
- If you do want to replace the older settings with MSN settings, click Yes.

Figure B.1 Tell the Sign In dialog box to remember your password (unless you're afraid that passers-by will use your computer to log in to MSN).

Other Ways to Connect

Clicking the Inbox icon on your desktop will start your e-mail program. If you use Microsoft Exchange, you can press CTRL-M or select Tools | Deliver Now to bring up the MSN Sign In dialog box.

If you use MSN to connect to the Internet, the Internet Explorer and other Web browsers, as well as other Internet programs, will automatically bring up the Sign In dialog box when you try to use them when not connected.

You can also create shortcuts to resources on MSN and place them on your desktop or in folders. Double-clicking such a shortcut will automatically start the process of connecting to MSN if you're not already connected.

Watching Your Connect Time

When you're connected to MSN, look in the right end of your status bar. A little MSN icon will appear there as long as you're connected. You can right-click on it as a shortcut to many MSN services. If you want to keep track of how long you're connected to MSN (after that free trial you'll pay a flat rate every month for 10 hours and then you'll pay by the hour after your quota is exceeded), you can double- click your modem icon in the status bar. A dialog box will appear, showing your connect time as it mountsl

MSN AND INTERNET E-MAIL

As soon as you connect to MSN, it will check to see if you've received any new mail, both from MSN and from the Internet (you may have to set up your mail program to make sure it can pick up your Internet mail, as explained in Chapter 4). MSN will notify you if you have any new mail.

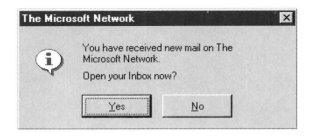

Click Yes to start your e-mail program. To send e-mail to any address on the Internet, just use the standard format for an Internet address: *username@internet.address.xyz*. To send mail to someone else on MSN, you can just specify their Member ID.

You can attach files (or shortcuts) to e-mail both to other MSN members and to Internet addresses. See Chapters 3 and 4 for more about Internet e-mail and Microsoft Exchange.

NAVIGATING MSN

Two other windows appear when you connect to MSN, a broadsheet of daily highlights and "events" on MSN, called MSN Today, and the main MSN window, which says The Microsoft Network in the title bar but is everywhere else referred to as MSN Central. Read MSN Today if you want or just close it (click the x button in the upper-right corner, as with any Windows 95 window). You can always bring it back by clicking the large MSN Today bar at the top of the MSN Central window (see Figure B.2).

The other four bars read E-Mail (it starts your e-mail program, just as when you first connected), Favorite Places (initially nothing, you put *your* favorites here), Member Assistance (help!), and Categories (bingo!). The Categories bar is the main way to get into the contents of MSN (at least until you've added some locations to your favorite places).

Click Categories. The window changes to the Categories window. MSN Categories windows all have a banner of some kind across the top. There are many varied categories of services and communication offered (see Figure B.3). You may have noticed that the Categories window replaced the MSN Central window when you clicked Categories. MSN windows are set to function this way by default (to avoid cluttering up your desktop), but you can select View | Options, click the Folder tab, click Browse folders using a separate window for each folder, and click OK.

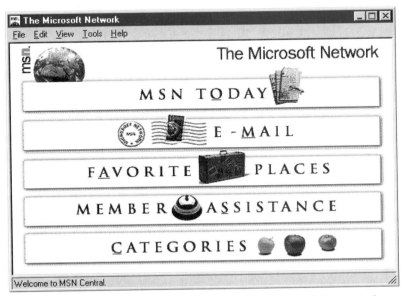

Figure B.2 MSN Central is the top level view of the Microsoft Network. Get started by clicking Categories.

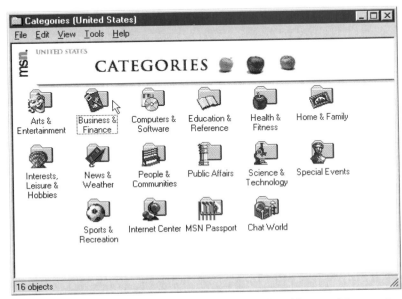

Figure B.3 Dig right into a folder and see what's offered in one of these categories.

The easiest way to "go back up" a level in MSN is to press BACKSPACE (yes, it's the same shortcut as is generally available for navigating windows in Windows 95). The menus can also be used to navigate, and all the most useful commands are repeated on the menus and the toolbars of each window.

If you prefer to see the whole "lay of the land" of MSN while browsing it, right-click on any icon and select Explore. You'll then get an Explorer-style window that will show you the "directory tree" in a left pane and the normal MSN window in the right.

It should be easy for you to get to whatever you want on MSN or the Internet. You shouldn't have to plow through many many folders within folders. So any time you find a folder or discussion area you enjoy, add it to your Favorite Places (select File | Add to Favorites) or make a shortcut from it (it will appear on your desktop). To make a shortcut from an icon, right-click on it and select Create Shortcut.

BULLETIN BOARDS (AND NEWSGROUPS)

The main form of interaction with other people on MSN is in the many BBSes. BBSes are areas where running conversations are posted. Anyone can read and reply to any message, adding to the conversation. You can also attach files to BBS messages, just as you can e-mail messages. In fact, the type of window you read and write BBS messages in is a lot like an e-mail window (see Figure B.4).

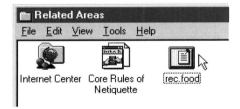

MSN presents Usenet newsgroups in exactly the same types of icons and windows, so once you know how to participate in BBSes, you know how to work with newsgroups too. Chapter 7 has more on reading Usenet news from MSN. Be aware of whether you're talking to just other MSN members or to a newsgroup with readers all over the Internet.

Many MSN Categories also include an Internet icon called Related Areas. Related Areas contains shortcuts to Internet resources and newsgroups on related subjects.

CHAT ROOMS AND MSN EVENTS

The other forum for communicating with others on MSN is the Chat Rooms. Chat Rooms are places where live, typed conversations are carried on, much like IRC on the Internet (see Chapter 8). A Chat Room window has three panes: a large one for the conversation, a pane on the right side listing the people involved in the conversation, and the horizontal pane on the bottom where you can see what you're typing.

THE REST OF THE NET: WEB, GOPHER AND FTP

To explore the rest of the Internet, such as the World Wide Web, Gopherspace, and the many FTP archive sites out there, you'll need to use a Web browser, such as Internet Explorer (the one that comes with the Microsoft Plus! Pack) or Netscape Navigator (the most widely distributed browser). MSN *could* have all kinds of useful shortcuts to Web, Gopher, and FTP sites, but as of late 1995, it does not. If you

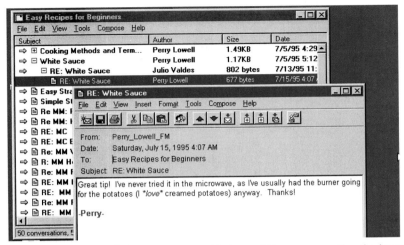

Figure B.4 Double-click on a message title to read the message. Use the buttons in the toolbar to reply, follow-up, or move to the next or previous message or conversation.

double-click an Internet shortcut, it will launch your Web browser, either Internet Explorer, or whichever browser you've installed more recently.

SEARCHING MSN

Another way to find content on MSN is to search for it; you can either select Start | Find | On The Microsoft Network or right-click the MSN icon in the status bar and select Find. A Find dialog box will appear. Type a word to search for and press ENTER or click Find Now. As with the "local" Windows 95 Find feature, a window opens in the bottom of the dialog box and items will start appearing in the window as they are found. Double-click on an item to go to it (or open it) directly.

FAVORITE PLACES

If you add icons to your Favorite Places, you can check into your regular MSN hang-outs without gallivanting all around the many folders. A quick way to jump right to your Favorite Places window is to right-click the MSN icon in the status bar and select Go to Favorite Places from the menu that pops up.

SIGNING OFF MSN

To sign off the Microsoft Network, click the File menu in any window and select Sign Off. If you leave your computer or otherwise don't access MSN for five minutes, a window will appear asking you to click Yes if you want to stay connected. If you're not there or if you do nothing, then it will automatically sign you off.

The Busy Person's Links

This appendix recounts all the Internet addresses mentioned in this book (and a few extra), organized by topic. An electronic version of this appendix can be found at http://syx.com/x/busy/.

THE WORLD WIDE WEB

Resource	Address
WWW FAQ	http://www.boutell.com/faq
Netscape Navigator	http://home.netscape.com/
Internet Explorer	http://www.microsoft.com/
Yahoo (a directory of the Web)	http://yahoo.com/
Enterzone (a Web 'zine)	http://enterzone.berkeley.edu/enterzone.html
Project Gutenberg (a gopher site)	gopher://garnet.msen.com:70/11/stuff/gutenberg
news.announce.newusers (a newsgroup)	news://news.announce.newusers
mal's web of vicarious delusions	http://www.emf.net/~mal
Internet Underground Music Archive	http://www.iuma.com
NetSurfer Digest	http://www.netsurf.com/nsd/
Cool Site of the Day	http://cool.infi.net

E-MAIL AND MAILING LISTS

Resource	Address
Eudora	http://www.qualcomm.com/quest/freeware.html
Pegasus Mail	http://www.cuslm.ca/pegasus/index.htm
Mail Tools	http://charlotte.acns.nwu.edu/mailtools/
Publicly Accessible Mailing Lists	http://www.NeoSoft.com/internet/paml/bysubj.html

USENET NEWSGROUPS AND NEWSREADERS

Resource	Address
Usenet Info Center FAQ	http://sunsite.unc.edu/usenet-i/info-center-faq.html
Free Agent (and Agent)	http://www.webpress.net/forte/agent/
News Xpress	ftp://ftp.hk.super.net/pub/windows/Winsock-Utilities/
WinVN	ftp://ftp.ksc.nasa.gov/pub/win3/winvn
NewsWatcher (for the Mac)	ftp://ftp.acns.nwu.edu/pub/newswatcher/
Nuntius (for the Mac)	ftp://ftp.cit.cornell.edu/pub/mac/comm/test/Nuntius-archive-mirror/

IRC AND OTHER FORMS OF CHAT

Resource	Address
IRC FAQ	http://www.kei.com/irc.html
IRC Related Documents	http://ftp.acsu.buffalo.edu/irc/WWW/ircdocs.html
Undernet	http://www.undernet.org:8080/~cs93jtl/Undernet.html

Resource	Address
Undernet IRC FAQ	http://www.undernet.org:8080/~cs93jtl/underfaq/
IRC Servers List	http://www.funet.fi/pub/unix/irc/docs/server.lst
mIRC *and* WSIRC	ftp://cs-ftp.bu.edu/irc/clients/pc/windows
Netscape Chat	http://home.netscape.com/comprod/chat.html
Global Chat	ftp://he.net/pub/prospero/globalchat/windows/
Internet Phone User Directory	http://www.pulver.com/iphone/
CU-SeeMe Welcome Page	http://cu-seeme.cornell.edu/

FTP, TELNET, AND GOPHER

Resource	Address
WS_FTP	ftp://129.29.64.246/pub/msdos/
WinZip	http://www.winzip.com/winzip/download.html
Consummate Winsock Applications	http://cwsapps.texas.net/
WSGopher	ftp://dewey.tis.inel.gov/pub/wsgopher
Fetch (Macintosh FTP client)	http://www.dartmouth.edu/pages/softdev/fetch.html
NCSA Telnet (Macintosh)	http://www.ncsa.uiuc.edu/SDG/Software/Brochure/Overview/MacTelnet.overview.html
TurboGopher (Macintosh)	ftp://ftp.lanl.gov/pub/mac/gopher

INTERNET DIRECTORIES

Resource	Address
WWW Virtual Library, Subject Catalogue	http://www.w3.org/hypertext/DataSources/bySubject/Overview.html
WWW Virtual Library, by access method	http://www.w3org/hypertext/DataSources/ByAccess.html
Whole Internet Catalog	http://gnn.com/wic/
Global Network Navigator	http://nearnet.gnn.com/GNNhome.html
NCSA What's New	http://www.ncsa.uiuc.edu/SDG/Software/Mosaic/Docs/whats-new.html
Netscape What's New	http://home.netscape.com/home/whats-new.html
Internet Resources Meta-Index	http://www.ncsa.uiuc.edu/SDG/Software/Mosaic/MetaIndex.html
The Mother-of-all BBS	htt:p//www.cs.colorado.edu/homes/mcbryan/public_html/bb/summary.html
The InterNIC InfoGuide	http://www.internic.net/infoguide.html
The Magellan Internet Directory	http://www.mckinley.com/
Point	http://pointcom.com/
The JumpStation	http://www.stir.ac.uk/jsbin/js
Scott Yanoff's Internet Services List	http://www.w3.org/hypertext/DataSources/Yanoff.html

SEARCHING THE INTERNET

Resource	Address
InfoSeek	http://www2.infoseek.com
Lycos	http://lycos.cs.cmu.edu/
WebCrawler	http://webcrawler.com/
WWWW	http://www.cs.colorado.edu/home/mcbryan/WWWW.html
Inktomi	http://inktomi.berkeley.edu/query.html
DejaNews (Usenet search)	http://www.cs.colorado.edu/home/mcbryan/WWWW.html
List of Whois servers	ftp://sipb.mit.edu/pub/whois/whois-servers.list

PLACES TO START BROWSING THE WEB
Internet (and Windows 95)

Resource	Address
Internet Society	http://www.isoc.org/
EFF's Guide to the Internet	http://www.eff.org/papers/eegtti/eegttitop.html
Zen and the Art of the Internet	http://oingomth.uwc.edu/inetguide/Zen/zen-1.0_toc.html
The Consummate Winsock Apps List	http://cwsapps.texas.net/
Windows Internet Software	ftp://ftp.lightside.com/lightside/win/InternetSoftware/
Windows Win 95 TCP/IP PPP Internet Connectivity Instructions	http://www.erv.com/w95_ppp.htm
The Windows95 TCP/IP Setup FAQ	http://www.aa.net/~pcd/slp95faq.html
NetWatch	http://www.pulver.com/netwatch/

Window 95 (and Shareware)

Resource	Address
NetEx Windows95 Software Archive and Discussion Forums	http://www.netex.net/w95/
Win95-L Windows95 FAQ	http://walden.mo.net/~rymabry/95winfaq.html
Windows 95 FAQ	http://www.process.com/win95/win95faq.htm
Windows 95 Tips	Tricks and Undocumented Features
Windows95 Annoyances	http://ocf.berkeley.edu/~daaron/win95ann.html
Windows 95 Links	http://uptown.turnpike.net/W/Windows95/95links.htm
Virtual Software Library	http://vsl.cnet.com/

News

Resource	Address
Newspaper and Current Periodical Room	http://lcweb.loc.gov/global/ncp/ncp.html
Mercury Center	http://www.sjmercury.com/home.htm
NY Times Syndicate	http://nytsyn.com/
NY Times FAX	http://nytimesfax.com/
NandO.net	http://www.nando.net/
The Gate	http://www.sfgate.com/

U.S. Government

Resource	Address
The White House	http://www.whitehouse.gov/
Thomas	http://thomas.loc.gov/
Library of Congress	http://loc.gov/

Entertainment and Complete Wastes of Time

Resource	Address
Internet Movie Database	http://www.msstate.edu/movies/welcome.html/
50 Greatest Conspiracies	http://www.webcom.com:80/~conspire/
biancaTroll productions	http://bianca.com/btp/index.html
Useless WWW page	http://www.primus.com/staff/paulp/useless.html
The net.legends FAQ	gopher://dixie.aiss.uiuc.edu:6969/11/urban.legends/net.legends.FAQ
eye.NET—The stupid net.coverage media awards	http://www.interlog.com/eye/News/Eyenet/Awards.html
The Urban Legends gopher site	gopher://dixie.aiss.uiuc.edu:6969/11/urban.legends
Anagram generator	http://csugrad.cs.vt.edu/~eburke/anagrams.html

WEB PUBLISHING

Resource	Address
Hypertext Markup Language (HTML)	http://www.w3.org/hypertext/WWW/MarkUp/
HTML Quick Reference	http://kuhttp.cc.ukans.edu/lynx_help/HTML_quick.html
Style Guide for Online Hypertext	http://www.w3.org/hypertext WWW/Provider/Style/Overview.html
How Do They Do That with HTML?	http://www.nashville.net/~carl/htmlguide/index.html
HTML Tutorial	http://fire.clarkson.edu/doc/html/htut.html

Resource	Address
WWW & HTML Developer's JumpStation	http://oneworld.wa.com/htmldev/devpage/dev-page.html
rtftohtml	ftp://ftp.cray.com/src/WWWstuff/RTF/rtftohtml_overview.html
E-Publish (a Word and RTF converter)	http://www.stattech.com.au/
HTML Assistant FAQ	http://cs.dal.ca/ftp/htmlasst/htmlafaq.html
Internet Assistant for Word for Windows 95	http://www.microsoft.com/msoffice/freestuf/MSWord/download/ia/ia95/chcklist.htm

FINDING A SERVICE PROVIDER AND SETTING UP A CONNECTION

Resource	Address
Pobox (mail and Web forwarding service)	http://pobox.com
Internet Service Providers	http://www.tagsys.com/Providers/index.html
Winsock driver	http://papa.indstate.edu:8888/winsock-faq.html
MacPPP	http://www.compumedia.com:80/pub/Software/mac/MacPPP.sit.bin
InterSLIP	http://www.intercon.com/
Chameleon Netmanage	http://www.netmanage.com
Trumpet	http://www.trumpet.com.au/wsk/winsock.htm
SLiRP	http://www.blitzen.canberra.edu.au/slirp/
TIA	http://marketplace.com/tia
SLiRP/TIA FAQs and Related URLs	http://www.webcom.com/~llarrow/tiafaqs.html

Index

O

P

The Books to Use When There's No Time to Lose

Computer Fundamentals for Complicated Lives

Whether you set aside an *evening*, a *lunch hour*, or reach for a ***Busy People*** guide as you need it, you're guaranteed to save time with Windows 95 and its associated productivity applications. Organized for a quick orientation to Windows 95, Word, Excel, Access, and the Internet, each ***Busy People*** title offers exceptional time-saving features and has the right blend of vital skills and handy shortcuts that you must know to get a job done quickly and accurately. Full-color text make the going easy and fun.

Written by a busy person (like you!) with a skeptic's view of computing, these opinionated, well-organized, and authoritative books are all you'll need to master the important ins and outs of Windows 95 and other best-selling software releases—without wasting your precious hours!

**Windows 95
for Busy People**
by Ron Mansfield
$22.95 USA
ISBN: 0-07-882110-X
Available Now

**Word for Windows 95
for Busy People**
by Christian Crumlish
$22.95 USA
ISBN: 0-07-882109-6
Available Now

**Excel for Windows 95
for Busy People**
by Ron Mansfield
$22.95 USA
ISBN: 0-07-882111-8
Available Now

**The Internet
for Busy People**
by Christian Crumlish
$22.95 USA
ISBN: 0-07-882108-8
Available Now

**Access for Windows
95 for Busy People**
by Alan Neibauer
$22.95 USA
ISBN: 0-07-882112-6
Available Now

To Order, Call Toll Free 1-800-822-8158   OSBORNE

Leaders of the Pack

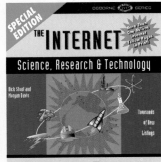

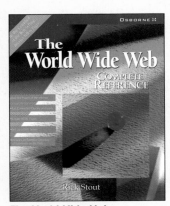